应用 SAS 实现
金融大数据研究

韩 燕◎著

USING SAS IN FINANCIAL BIG DATA RESEARCH

北京理工大学出版社
BEIJING INSTITUTE OF TECHNOLOGY PRESS

版权专有　侵权必究

图书在版编目（CIP）数据

应用 SAS 实现金融大数据研究：英文/韩燕著. —北京：北京理工大学出版社，2021.4
ISBN 978 – 7 – 5682 – 9737 – 0

Ⅰ.①应…　Ⅱ.①韩…　Ⅲ.①统计分析 – 应用软件 – 应用 – 金融 – 数据处理 – 英文　Ⅳ.①F830.41

中国版本图书馆 CIP 数据核字（2021）第 067390 号

出版发行 /	北京理工大学出版社有限责任公司
社　　址 /	北京市海淀区中关村南大街 5 号
邮　　编 /	100081
电　　话 /	（010）68914775（总编室）
	（010）82562903（教材售后服务热线）
	（010）68948351（其他图书服务热线）
网　　址 /	http：//www.bitpress.com.cn
经　　销 /	全国各地新华书店
印　　刷 /	三河市华骏印务包装有限公司
开　　本 /	710 毫米 × 1000 毫米　1/16
印　　张 /	10
字　　数 /	190 千字
版　　次 /	2021 年 4 月第 1 版　2021 年 4 月第 1 次印刷
定　　价 /	62.00 元

责任编辑 /	武丽娟
文案编辑 /	武丽娟
责任校对 /	刘亚男
责任印制 /	李志强

图书出现印装质量问题，请拨打售后服务热线，本社负责调换

Preface

Financial research relies extensively on data. Mastering a statistical tool capable of handling the huge quantity of financial data is a necessary technique for every financial empiricist. There are many such tools, for example, Matlab, Stata, R, SQL, Python, etc. As a veteran in the field of empirical financial research, I have been using SAS for quite a long time. During the long years of experience, I gradually start appreciating SAS's powerful yet smart ability to help me navigate through the ocean of financial data. I should admit that I have very limited, but not totally zero, knowledge of using other statistical software. However, I still feel obliged to compare SAS with other software in the context of financial research. The most distinguished advantage of SAS over other software is its ability to handle big data. This advantage is all the more meaningful when it comes to financial data. Let me explain this advantage as follows.

Big data analysis has become trendy during the past five to ten years, largely due to the rapid development of IT technology. To analyze data, we need to find the data in the first place. In this regard, financial data has long been collected, compiled, and distributed in a systematic, thorough, and scientific way. Most of the financial data originate from exchanges and the companies' legally published periodic reports. In many countries, the financial information is universally formatted. These features make the financial data most easily to be collected and converted into commercial database. Many companies provide such database, such as WRDS, Thomson Reuters, CSMAR, and WIND. The Nobel laureate, Professor Eugene Fama, once mentioned that he had started using WRDS database to conduct researches since 1970s. In this sense, big data has been in place in financial research for about half a century, long ahead of the recent boom of big data analysis. To some degree, the financial data define the research topics, methodologies, and even sub-disciplines of today's financial research.

According to my personal observation, the researchers' choice of the statistical software in the business and economics schools in universities varies from school to school. Interestingly, those in the finance departments are more likely to choose SAS, while those in economics and econometrics are more likely to choose Stata. This pattern of choice does have a reason. SAS treats data as a table, which stores and processes data line by line. Therefore, SAS theoretically has unlimited ability to dealing with any number of lines, although it necessarily takes a long time once the data are prohibitively large. In contrast, Stata treats data as a matrix, which requires, at least in theory, to read all data into the computer's memory before starts the processing. This way, Stata's ability to handle data is only as powerful as the computer's memory size. However, Stata's treating data as a matrix has a deeper rationale. That is, most modern econometric models are expressed in matrices, which means processing data in the form of a matrix is a more natural way in econometric research context. Partly due to this reason, when my students ask me why I choose SAS over Stata, I often half seriously and half jokingly answer them: "That is because I am not an econometrician."

I can add another interesting observation to corroborate my argument that econometricians and those with strong econometric backgrounds tend to choose Stata. The similar choice pattern also shows up in the students who learn their econometric courses taught by the professors with different backgrounds. Empirical research methods have been compulsory courses in many business, economics, and finance programs at undergraduate, graduate, and doctoral levels in many universities. However, the professors teaching econometric have different backgrounds. In many schools, it is the econometric professor who teaches the students the concepts and methodologies of empirical research, no matter the students major in econometric or not. Needless to say, econometricians' teaching econometrics can provide the most advanced, thorough, and rigorous knowledge of the field to the students. But when it comes to the application of empirical research methods on a specific economics or finance question, the researchers in that particular field typically have a specific preference of certain econometric methods. Often the case, top tier economics and finance journals reject the papers whose main contribution is merely to apply a "better" econometric method to an old research question. In other words, high quality economics and finance research puts more weight on ideas over econometric techniques. Therefore, there has gradually emerged a new norm in which the econometric course is taught by an economic or finance professor who does not major in econometrics, statistics, or math, but specializes in specific research areas. Over the past years, I have been teaching and working with many students. It seems that those who learn econometrics from professors majoring in econometrics tend to choose Stata, while those who learn econometrics from professors majoring in finance tend to choose SAS.

Given that SAS does not treat data as matrices, it seems to lose to Stata in terms of timely incorporating the newest statistical mythologies into the software. But on the flip side, the nearly unlimited ability to process any number of lines of data does make SAS more suitable, and in certain studies the only choice, for financial research. Those who have no experiences in handling financial data may not fully appreciate the massive quantity of financial data. Let me put it in perspective. Compared to the U.S. financial market, Chinese financial market has a very short history. We have just celebrated the thirtieth anniversary of the Chinese stock market as I finish writing this book. However, there have been more than 47 million trading-day observations for all Chinese bonds, and more than 11 million trading day observations for all Chinese stocks. For the microstructure (tick-by-tick) data, the number of observations is thousands of times larger than the daily data. The exceedingly large size of financial posts a series of challenges to us. For example, sorting data is a routine process. However, most of personal computers will have difficulty in sorting a data set with hundreds of millions of data by several variables. Matching data is another simple yet challenging task for Big data. The typical way of matching data is to first use a Cartesian product and then eliminate those that are not matched. A Cartesian product of two tables with x and y lines generate a x times y lines temporary table. Imagine how daunting the task could be if you are trying to match two tables which both have 10 million lines. In these scenarios, we need to find smarter ways to conduct the data processing. Fortunately, SAS can provide many handy tools for us.

This book summarizes my experience in using SAS to conduct financial research on big data. One of my research areas is market microstructure, which studies the tick-by-tick data of trades and quotes. As mentioned above, market microstructure data are especially large, hence a more demanding task for researchers. I often wait for a whole day to get one result. Although often frustrated and disappointed by the tedious calculation process, I have learned a lot from these studies. Most of all, I gradually master the skills that enable me to decipher the regularities hidden in the tremendous amount of data. There are many books discussing how to use SAS. I do not intend to add to this long list. This book is rather focused on how to use SAS to conduct sophisticated financial researches, especially in the context of big data. I assume that the readers have already understood the basics of SAS. The topics of this book mainly cover the advanced research and coding issues that are seldomly discussed in the general-purpose and introductory-level SAS books. I hope the experience shared in this book can be of some help for you to conduct high-quality financial researches.

Han Yan was supported by the National Natural Science Foundation of China under grant number 71772013.

Contents

1 Basic Rules when Using SAS ·········· 1
   1.1 Build Our Own Research Database ·········· 1
   1.2 Importing and Exporting Data ·········· 2
   1.3 Managing Libraries and Data Sets ·········· 5
   1.4 Enhancing SAS Efficiency ·········· 8
   1.5 Best Practice to Make Our Codes and Data More Robust ·········· 10

2 Advanced Usage of SAS ·········· 13
   2.1 Loops and Arrays ·········· 13
   2.2 BY statement ·········· 16
   2.3 Lag and Dif ·········· 17
   2.4 Date and Times Formats and Informats ·········· 20
   2.5 PROC MEANS ·········· 21

3 Manipulating Tables ... 25
- 3.1 Concatenating Tables ... 26
- 3.2 Merging Tables in SQL procedure ... 29
- 3.3 Merging Tables in DATA Step Using MERGE Statement ... 33
- 3.4 Modifying Tables ... 34
- 3.5 Transposing Tables ... 36
- 3.6 Subsetting Tables ... 37

4 SAS Macros ... 39
- 4.1 Understanding the Basics of SAS Macros ... 39
- 4.2 How SAS Executes a Macro ... 41
- 4.3 The Coding Rules in Macros That are Different From Other SAS Codes ... 43
- 4.4 Return The Total Number of Observations ... 44
- 4.5 Existence of A Macro Variable and The Zero Observation of A Dataset ... 46

5 Using SAS to Execute Financial Research Methodologies ... 49
- 5.1 Storing Results Generate by SAS Procedures ... 49
- 5.2 Summarizing Data and Statistical Tests ... 50
- 5.3 Regressions ... 53
- 5.4 Simulation Methods ... 57
- 5.5 Event Studies ... 61

6 Research on Mutual Funds ... 71
- 6.1 The Major Research Questions in Mutual Fund Studies ... 71
- 6.2 Calculating Fund Returns ... 77
- 6.3 Calculating Fund Alpha's Using a Macro ... 81
- 6.4 Calculating Fund Flows ... 84

7 Market Microstructure Research ... 93
7.1 Research on Decomposing Bid-ask Spread and Estimating PIN ... 93
7.2 Estimating the Microstructure Measures ... 98
参考文献 ... 141

1

Basic Rules when Using SAS

This book is not intended to be a manual or introductory book of SAS. Readers are assumed to have reasonable knowledge and/or experiences of SAS. When more than one method is present to accomplish the same goal, the author offers only one method, partly because of the lack of knowledge, partly because being thorough is by no means the aim of this book.

1.1 Build Our Own Research Database

A research project may last several months, or several years at the most. But as academia, our researches last as long as our career. Often the time, we will find the coding work highly repetitive. Take the following example. In reality, fund management firms usually launch different mutual fund products in order to cater to the needs of different customers. For example, different classes. But for most studies in mutual funds, these different classes of funds should be treated as one fund. Therefore, an important job is to identify the unique fund. Every time we launch a mutual fund research project, we need to do this. Apparently, it saves us a lot of time if we can gradually build our database. We don't want to redo everything.

It's common that multiple researchers work together on one project. So collaborating becomes vital in terms of research efficiency. It is extremely rare that everyone in the research team is using the same software and the same computer. A very common scenario is that someone is using SAS on a Windows computer, someone is using SAS on Mac computers, and someone is using Stata etc. To make the things even more complicated, once the data contain non-English characters, the coding becomes vital. Therefore, it is a good practice to always require the codes and data are compiled in UTF-8 format. This can be done through a special clause in the Libname command.

1.2 Importing and Exporting Data

Finance research usually uses readily compiled data. These data are typically from some data providers, such as WRDS, CSMAR, and RESSET. So the first job of finance research is to "get these data into SAS." A typical way is to download the data from the data provider's website, and then to import the data into our libraries. An atypical way is to directly access the data on the data provider's database as long as such service is provided by the provider. The following summarizes the best practice of importing data.

First, check the properties of the variables. If a variable contains both numeric values and character values, some of the values, especially the numeric values are likely to be ignored. For example, if SAS has assigned the column to be numeric, then all the characters will not be imported. To avoid this problem, first in the excel file, add a character, say $ to every cell of the column, then import the file, then in SAS, modify the imported file using the following code.

```
Variablename = substr(variablename,2);
```

Then we can import the original data into SAS. Depending on the formats of the original data, we may choose one of the following codes.

To import delimited/CSV files, we can use:

```
proc import
    datafile ='a:\..\filename.txt'
    out      =tnfdata
    dbms     =dlm(or csv)
    replace;
    Delimiter ='#';
    Getnames =yes;
run;
```

To import Excel files, we can use:

```
proc import
    datafile = '/folders/myshortcuts/Downloads/abc_export.xlsx'
    out =work.x1 dbms =xlsx replace;
    datarow =3;
    sheet ='Sheet1';
    Getnames =no;
run;
```

To import aligned txt files, we can use: (The input file shouldn't contain the headers.)

```
Data   test.ffm (drop = dt);
  infile    'c:\ffm.txt';
  input     dt   $
       Mkt_RF   SMB   HML   RF;
  Date = intnx('month', Input (cats(dt,'01'), anydtdte11.),
0, 'end');
  format  Date  date9.;
  Mkt_RF = Mkt_RF /100;
  SMB = SMB /100;
  HML = HML /100;
  RF = RF /100;
run;
```

The following codes can import a large variety of files, for example csv, txt, and bcp. Just specify the correct file name and extension, there is no need to change other parts of the codes. The extension is enough to tell SAS what type of file we are importing. Notice how the following codes import time. If the date and time are in "good shape," then the following is the best way to import date and time variables. If they are not in good shape, then we have to import them in character form and then use other functions to convert them into date and time. "Good shape" entails us to find the correct information.

```
    data work.abc_import;
      %let _EFIERR_ = 0; /* set the ERROR detection macro variable */
        infile '/…/abc.csv'
          MISSOVER DSD lrecl =32767 firstobs =2 delimiter ='|';
```

```
    length STKCD $ 12.;
    length CONAME $180.;
    length FYENDDT $12.;
    length FYREPORT_IND $ 16.;
    input RANO STKCD $ CONAME $ FYENDDT $ FYREPORT_IND $;
    if_ERROR_then call symputx('_EFIERR_',1);
run;
```

In the above codes, lrecl = 32,767 specifies the length and the location, so there is no need to change them. Pay attention to delimiter and firstobs options. The delimiter option specifies the delimiter. The firstobs option specifies from which line to import the data. So if the data contain a header, then firstobs = 2, otherwise, firstobs = 1. When the original data contain a header, and we want to change the variable name, there is no need to "change" the variable name. Just specifying a different name in the input option will do, because firstobs = 2 instructs SAS to ignore the header, and the input option specifies the variable name in the SAS data, hence the header in the original data has no role in importing. The only role of the header is to "remind" us how to name the variables.

1.3 Managing Libraries and Data Sets

We can protect a data set by assigning a password to the data set. SAS has three types of password: read, write, and alter. For protecting a data set against others to alter a data set, assign write and alter password to it. For example:

```
    data test.datasetpw (write = password alter = password);
set csmar.cf_fdatvaln; run;
```

```
proc sort data = test.datasetpw (write = password alter = 
password); by netu; run;
    proc datasets library = mylib; modify students(write = 
password alter = password); run;
```

The first line of codes define a new data set with write and alter password protection. The second line of codes sorts an existing data set, which either has already been assigned passwords or has not been assigned passwords and is assigned by these codes now.

To delete a password, use the following codes:

```
proc datasets library = cnmarket nolist;
modify dailymarketreturn (read = abc/);
```

Note that the above codes remove the read protection of data set "cnmarket. dailymarketreturn," which has been formerly assigned to a password of abc. And do not forget the slash followed by the password. Notice that SAS password protection does not prevent the data set from being deleted in Windows Explorer.

Use the following codes to re-order variables in the current data set.

```
data dataset-name;
  retain var1 var2;
  set dataset-name;
run;
```

Notice that the variables following RETAIN statement will appear in the first place. Variables not appeared after RETAIN statement will appear in the same order as they were.

Then let us look at how to copy a data set to another library. Say there are two libraries: liba, libb. There is a data set name dataone in liba. The following program copies this data set into libb.

```
Proc datasets library = libb;
Copy in = liba out = libb;
Select dataone;
Run;
```

Notice that the new data set in libb has the same name as the one in liba. And the above program has the same effects with the following program:

```
Data libb.dataone;
Set liba.dataone;
Run;
```

Sometimes, we want to list library and dataset. The following codes list all the files in a library:

```
Proc datasets library = MyLibName;
Proc datasets library = MyLibName memtype = data;
```

The latter line of codes instructs SAS to show only files of data member type (another member type of SAS files is CATALOG).

The following codes list the information of data sets:

```
Proc datasets library = MyLibName; contents data = MyDatasetName;

Proc datasets library = MyLibName; contents data = _all_;
```

The following codes list the data sets in a library and output the list to a new data set.

```
ods output Members = work.members;
proc datasets memtype = data library = res_sas; run; quit;
```

1.4 Enhancing SAS Efficiency

As we have discussed, one advantage of SAS is its ability to handle very large data. For small data sets, the efficiency of SAS coding does not make a big difference. But it is not the case when the data set is large. It is quite common in finance researches that the data set is very large. For data sets of big size, different coding may mean hours or maybe days of difference in execution time. Furthermore, SAS may fail in executing some codes on large data sets. For example, it is usually impossible to sort a data set with more than tens of millions of observations. In these circumstances, we need to find ways to improve coding efficiency in order to save execution time and make the impossible possible.

The followings are some of the methods we can consider to use. Before considering the following methods, one should keep in mind this caveat. There is no guarantee that the following methods always increase the efficiency. They may cause much longer execution time.

One way to enhance SAS efficiency is to keep a dataset in memory. When SAS executes the codes, it usually needs to read the data sets into memory before it starts to process each observation of the data set. When the execution of a section of the code has finished, i. e. , all observations have been read and processed, the data set will be dumped out of the memory. So if the code repeatedly calls one or more data sets, it may be more efficient to tell SAS to keep the file in memory.

Use the following to keep a dataset or a library in the memory:

```
sasfile test.a open;
```

Use the following to close.

```
sasfile test.a close;
```

Another way to consider in order to enhance SAS efficiency is to reassign location of utility files. Sometimes the default disk doesn't have enough space for the utility files, then a new location needs to be assigned. Use the following codes to achieve this.

```
UTILLOC ='/sastemp/bit_HY';
```

When running SAS on Unix server, use the following way to reassign the work and utility files. When submit the SAS codes, use this statement line:

```
sas-work/research/bit_HY/worklib   mycodes.sas
```

Or

```
sas  -work···/worklib   mycodes.sas
```

Indexing is the third way to enhance SAS efficiency. It is especially useful when we are merging and finding data entries. There are two ways to creating an index or indexes: using the PROC DATASETS procedure, or using the INDEX = Data Set Option.

The DATASETS procedure provides statements that enable us to create and delete indexes. In the following example, the MODIFY statement identifies the data file, the INDEX DELETE statement deletes two indexes, and the two INDEX CREATE statements specify the variables to index, with the first INDEX CREATE statement specifying the options UNIQUE and NOMISS:

```
proc datasets library=mylib;
modify employee;
   index delete salary age;
   index delete _all_;
   index create empnum /unique nomiss;
   index create names =(lastname frstname);
```

Note that if we delete and create indexes in the same step, place the INDEX

DELETE statement before the INDEX CREATE statement so that space occupied by deleted indexes can be reused during index creation.

To create indexes in a DATA step when we create the data file, use the INDEX = data set option. The INDEX = data set option also enables us to include the NOMISS and UNIQUE options. The following example creates a simple index on the variable STOCK and specifies UNIQUE:

```
data finances(index = (stock /unique));
```

The next example uses the variables SSN, CITY, and STATE to create a simple index named SSN and a composite index named CITYST:

```
data employee(index = (ssn cityst = (city state)));
```

Note that the INDEX option cannot appear in the SET statement.

1.5 Best Practice to Make Our Codes and Data More Robust

In SAS, a name should begin with a character or an underscore, and no special characters except for the underscores, are allowed. It is not a good practice to assign a much long name. The maximum length are 32 characters. The following SAS language elements require a bit more restrictively:

Engines, Filerefs, Librefs, and Passwords require no more than 8 characters;

CALL routines, Functions, and Procedure names require no more than 16 characters.

If we have to include spaces (blanks) or special characters in a name, we can use SAS name literals, which is a string of characters enclosed by quotations marks, and is followed by character n. For example:

```
Input 'Bob's Asset Number'n
X_variable = ('Amount Budgeted 'n 'Amount Spent'n)
```

Rules for quotation marks are worth mentioning. Use quotation mark to enclose a string of characters. If the string of characters contains a quotation mark, the double quotation mark should be used. For example:

```
'Buffet"s Secrets'
```

If the length of a variable is not explicitly defined, then SAS assigns to it the length of the first observation of this variable. So if later observations have more length than the first one, these values would be incomplete. To circumvent this problem, explicitly define the length of the variable, using codes like the following:

```
Data MyDataSetName; set MySourceDataSetName; length NewVarName $ 15; if condition1 then NewVarName = 'no'; else NewVarName = 'yes'; run;
```

In a SQL procedure, use the following to define the length:

```
Proc sql;
   Create table ... as
   Select a.name as name length =18, a.time, ...
   ...
```

2

Advanced Usage of SAS

2.1 Loops and Arrays

Loops is a very common feature in every computer coding, including SAS. It is very helpful to create the repetitive codes, by reducing errors, quick altering codes, etc. There are several ways to create loops. The most important codes is DO statement.

```
data work.x;
   do i =1 to 10;
      output;
   end;
run;
```

To define a simple or a multidimensional array, use the ARRAY statement. The ARRAY statement has the following form:

```
ARRAY array-name {number-of-elements} <list-of-variables>;
array books{3} Reference Usage Introduction;
array days{7} D1-D7;
array c1temp{*} c1t1 c1t2 c1t3 c1t4 c1t5;
array c1t{5};
array temprg{2,5} c1t1-c1t5 c2t1-c2t5;
```

The last code defines an array with 2 rows and 5 columns.

To understand the benefits of using DO Loops to selected elements of an array, let us look at the following examples. Say we have defined the array using the following code:

```
array days{7} D1-D7;
```

Then

```
do i=2 to 4;
```

processes elements 2 through 4

```
do i=1 to 7 by 2;
```

processes elements 1, 3, 5, and 7

```
do i=3,5;
```

processes elements 3 and 5.

An array definition is in effect only for the duration of the DATA step. If we want to use the same array in several DATA steps, we must redefine the array in each step. Before we make any references to an array, an ARRAY statement must appear in the same DATA step that we used to create the array. We can also use the special array subscript asterisk (*) to refer to all variables in an array in an INPUT or PUT statement or in the argument of a function.

Sometimes we need a way to determine the number of elements in an array. Use DIM function to determine the number of elements in an array. The form of DIM function is as follows:

```
DIMn(array-name)
```

For example:

```
Do i =1 to DIM(days);
Do i =1 to DIM4(days);
```

Multidimensional arrays are usually processed inside nested DO loops. As an example, the following is one form that processes a two-dimensional array:

```
DO index-variable-1 =1 TO number-of-rows;
 DO index-variable-2 =1 TO number-of-columns;
 ...more SAS statements...
 END;
END;
```

Arrays are often processed in iterative DO loops that use the array reference in a DO WHILE or DO UNTIL expression. In this example, the iterative DO loop processes the elements of the array named TREND.

```
data test;
    array trend{5} x1-x5;
    input x1-x5 y;
    do i =1 to 5 while(trend{i} <y);
    ...more SAS statements...
    end;
    datalines;
...data lines...
;
```

2.2 BY statement

BY statement is very important because it can repeat the process within each group identified by the variables following BY statement. BY statement looks like this:

BY variable(s);

BY < DESCENDING > variable(s) < NOTSORTED >
   < GROUPFORMAT >;

where DESCENDING indicates that the data sets are sorted in descending order (largest to smallest) by the variable that is specified. If we have more than one variable in the BY group, DESCENDING applies only to the variable that immediately follows it. NOTSORTED specifies that observations with the same BY value are grouped together but are not necessarily stored in alphabetical or numeric order.

We can invoke BY-group processing in both DATA steps and PROC steps by using a BY statement. Before we process one or more SAS data sets using grouped or ordered data with the SET, MERGE, or UPDATE statements, we must check the data to determine if they require preprocessing. If the observations are not in the order that we want, we must either sort the data set or create an index for it before using BY-group processing.

A preprocessing using BY statement involves sorting or indexing the data. So it is a good practice to sort observations for BY-group processing. We can use the SORT procedure to change the physical order of the observations in the data set. For example:

```
proc sort data = information;
    by State ZipCode;
run;
```

2.3 Lag and Dif

When used in the simplest way, LAG and DIF act as lag and difference functions. However, it is important to keep in mind that, despite their names, the LAG and DIF functions available in the DATA step are not true LAG and DIF functions.

Rather, LAG and DIF are queuing functions that remember and return argument values from previous calls. The LAG function remembers the value we pass to it and returns as its result the value we passed to it on the previous call. The DIF function works the same way but returns the difference between the current argument and the remembered value. (LAG and DIF return a missing value the first time the function is called.)

A true lag function does not return the value of the argument for the "previous call," as do the DATA step LAG and DIF functions. Instead, a true LAG function returns the value of its argument for the "previous observation," regardless of the sequence of previous calls to the function. Thus, for a true LAG function to be possible, it must be clear what the "previous observation" is.

If the data are sorted chronologically, then LAG and DIF act as true LAG and DIF functions. If in doubt, use PROC SORT to sort our data prior to using the LAG and DIF functions. Beware of missing observations, which may cause LAG and DIF to return values that are not the actual LAG and DIF values.

The DATA step is a powerful tool that can read any number of observations from any number of input files or data sets, can create any number of output data sets, and can write any number of output observations to any of the output data sets, all in the same program. Thus, in general, it is not clear what "previous observation" means in a DATA step program. In a DATA step program, the "previous observation" exists only if we write the program in a simple way that makes this concept meaningful.

Since, in general, the previous observation is not clearly defined, it is not possible to make true LAG or DIF functions for the DATA step. Instead, the DATA step provides queuing functions that make it easy to compute lags and differences.

The LAG and DIF functions compute lags and differences provided that the sequence of calls to the function corresponds to the sequence of observations in the output data set. However, any complexity in the DATA step that breaks this correspondence causes the LAG and DIF functions to produce unexpected results.

For example, suppose we want to add the variable CPILAG to the USCPI data set, as in the previous example, and we also want to subset the series to 1991 and later years. We might use the following statements:

```
data subset;
   set uscpi;
   if date > = '1jan1991'd;
   cpilag = lag(cpi);   /* WRONG PLACEMENT. */
run;
```

If the subsetting IF statement comes before the LAG function call, the value of CPILAG will be missing for January 1991, even though a value for December 1990 is available in the USCPI data set. To avoid losing this value, we must rearrange the statements to ensure that the LAG function is actually executed for the December 1990 observation.

```
data subset;
  set uscpi;
  cpilag = lag(cpi);
  if date >= '1jan1991'd;
run;
```

In other cases, the subsetting statement should come before the LAG and DIF functions. For example, the following statements subset the FOREOUT data set shown in a previous example to select only _TYPE_ = RESIDUAL observations and also to compute the variable LAGRESID.

```
data residual;
  set foreout;
  if _type_ = "RESIDUAL";
  lagresid = lag(cpi);
run;
```

Another pitfall of LAG and DIF functions arises when they are used to process time series cross-sectional data sets. For example, suppose we want to add the variable CPILAG to the CPICITY data set shown in a previous example. We might use the following statements:

```
data cpicity;
  set cpicity;
  cpilag = lag(cpi);
run;
```

However, these statements do not yield the desired result. In the data set produced by these statements, the value of CPILAG for the first observation for the first city is missing (as it should be), but in the first observation for all later cities, CPILAG contains the last value for the previous city. To correct this, set the lagged variable to missing at the start of each cross section, as follows:

```
data cpicity;
  set cpicity;
  by city date;
  cpilag = lag( cpi );
  if first.city then cpilag = .;
run;
```

2.4 Date and Times Formats and Informats

SAS stores date and times in the forms of integers. So it is very important to smartly use the formats and informats of date and times. Table 1 shows the date and datetime formats that are often used in SAS.

Table 1 Date and datetime format

ID values	Periodicity	Format	Example
SAS Date	Annual	YEAR4.	1991
	Quarterly	YYQC6.	1991:4
	Monthly	MONYY7.	OCT1991
	Weekly	WEEKDATX23.	Thursday, 17 Oct 1991
		DATE9.	17OCT1991
	Daily	DATE9.	17OCT1991
SAS Datetime	Hourly	DATETIME10.	17OCT91:14
	Minutes	DATETIME13.	17OCT91:14:45
	Seconds	DATETIME16.	17OCT91:14:45:32

Readers who have used SAS for some time may be familiar with how to write date constants and time constants separately. However, in some research scenarios, especially market microstructure studies, using datetime is a better choice. Table 2 shows how to write datetime constants.

Table 2　Examples of writing datetime constants

Datetime Constant	Time
17OCT1991:14:45:32'DT	32 seconds past 2:45 p.m., 17 October 1991
17OCT1991:12:5'DT	12:05 p.m., 17 October 1991
17OCT1991:2:0'DT	2:00 a.m., 17 October 1991
17OCT1991:0:0'DT	midnight, 17 October 1991

When dealing with date, INTCK function is very useful. For example, to assign an annual serial number but the year ending at 31 July, use the following codes:

```
int(intck('month','01aug2007'd,b.date)/12) as yrmnth
```

Notice the following: 1) do not use round function. 2) the starting date, i.e., 01aug2007 in the above example, should be earlier than the date. In other words, the assigned period number should be positive. 3) the first time parameters in the intck function is earlier than the second parameter. 4) in the above example, because using 'month', '01aug' is the same as '15aug' or '30aug'.

2.5　PROC MEANS

PROC MEANS is more than summarizing data. It is very useful in financial research, for example calculating the portfolio returns, either equally weighted or value weighted. The following is an example of PROC MEANS.

```
proc means data = work.a noprint;
output out = work._b( drop = _type_ _freq_)
mean( var1 var2 var3 ) = Mean1 Mean2 Mean3 Var( var3 var4 ) = Variance3 Variance4;
by by_variable;
weight weight_variable;
run;
```

If we omit the NOTSORTED option in the BY statement, then the observations in the data set either must be sorted by all the variables that we specify or must be indexed appropriately. We do not have to sort the data by class variables. Statistic keyword specifies which statistic to store in the output data set. See Table 3 for the available statistic keywords.

Table 3 Statistics keywords offered in PROC MEANS

Descriptive statistics keyword	
CSS	RANGE
CV	SKEWNESS | SKEW
KURTOSIS | KURT	STDDEV | STD
LCLM	STDERR
MAX	SUM
MEAN	SUMWGT
MIN	UCLM
N	USS
NMISS	VAR
Quantile statistics keyword	
MEDIAN | P50	Q3 | P75
P1	P90
P5	P95

续表

Quantile statistics keyword	
P10	P99
Q1 | P25	QRANGE
Hypothesis testing keyword	
PROBT	T

3

Manipulating Tables

Although the aim of using SAS is to analyze the data, most of the jobs in finance research is to prepare the data for the statistical analyses. Among the preparation work, connecting different tables is usually an important job. That is because to prepare the data is to collect the data from different tables and sources into one table. In this chapter, we are going to discuss different methods of connecting tables.

Generally speaking, there are two types of connecting tables: concatenating and merging. Concatenating two tables means putting one table to the end of another table. In this process, the newly created table becomes longer, but is typically as wide as one of the component tables. Merging two tables means putting the two tables side by side. In this process, the newly created table becomes wider, but typically has the same length as one of the component tables. Surely, there are many variants to the two types described above. But in essence, these two types of connecting tables cover virtually all the cases in finance researchs.

3.1 Concatenating Tables

There are three ways to concatenate tables: SET statement, APPEND procedure, and SQL OUTER UNION CORR statement.

Using SET statement to concatenate tables is straightforward. Preferably, the tables to be concatenated should share at least some common variables. However, it is by no means a requirement. We can concatenate data sets with completely different variables as long as it makes sense to do so. When SAS concatenate tables, it first list all the variables in all the tables to be concatenated. Then the newly created table has all these variables. But note that if one or more common variables have different attributes, for example different labels or formats, SAS may issue a warning.

It is very simple to concatenate data sets using SET statement:

```
data work.concatenated;
 set work.component1
        work.component2
        work.component3;
run;
```

The benefit of using SET statement to concatenate tables is that it can concatenate more than two tables. During the concatenation, we can further process the data, such as creating new variables, controlling the observations read into the SET statement, etc. Moreover, if each of the component tables is sorted by the same set of variables, we can add the BY statement in order to get the concatenated table also sorted by the same variables. For example:

```
data work.all_panels;
  set work.panel_2018
      work.panel_2019
      work.panel_2020;
  by stkcd date;
run;
```

This feature is very useful in the following scenario. Assume we have a very large data set, which renders direct sorting impossible. We can split the data set into several parts; sort each part; concatenate all the sorted parts; and get the sorted concatenated data set.

Besides the SET statement, we can also use APPEND procedure to concatenate two data sets using. Notice that APPEND procedure concatenates only two data sets, while SET statement can handle any number of data sets. The APPEND procedure has the following form:

```
proc append base = work.base_data_set data = work.new_part force;
run;
```

In the above program, work. new_part will be added to the end of work. base_data_set. Assume work. base_data_set has 100 observations, and work. new_part has 30 observations. Then after execution of this program, work. base_data_set has 130 observations.

Note the FORCE option in the APPEND procedure. If the data sets have different variables or some common variables have different attributes, then the procedure will not run properly until we include the FORCE option in the code. The effect of including FORCE option is slightly different from the result of SET statement in DATA process. When FORCE is used, the base data set will prevail in the sense that the variables that are present in work. new_part but not in work. base_data_set will be discarded. Interested readers can use the following codes to check how the FORCE option works.

```
data work.ab work.ac;
  a =1; output;
run;
data work.b;
  b =2; output;
run;
data work.c;
  a =3; c =4; output;
run;
proc append base =work.ab data =work.b force; run;
proc append base =work.ac data =work.c force; run;
```

The advantage of using APPEND rather than SET is its efficiency, because SET statement instructs SAS to process all the observations in the data sets, while APPEND procedure simply append the observations to the base data set without processing the observations in the base data set. This advantage is desirable when the base data set is very large.

The third way to concatenate tables is to use SQL OUTER UNION CORR statement. Take the following codes as an example.

```
data work.ab;
  a =1; b =2; output;
run;
data work.ac;
  a =2; c =3; output;
run;
```

```
proc sql;
  create table work.d as
  (select a from work.ab)
  outer union corr
  (select a from work.ac);

  create table work.e as
  (select b from work.ab)
  outer union corr
  (select a, c from work.ac)
  order by c desc;

  create table work.f as
  (select b, 'ab' as from_where from work.ab)
  outer union corr
  (select a, c, 'ac' as from_where from work.ac)
  order by from_where;
quit;
```

The advantage of using SQL OUTER UNION CORR statement is that it provides more freedom of controlling the variables and orders in the newly created table. Notice the creation of table work. f in the above code. This table has a new variable "from_where" to indicate the source of the observations in work. f. This variable can be created neither by SET statement nor by APPEND procedure.

3.2 Merging Tables in SQL procedure

Merging tables is a much more common job than concatenating tables in finance research. There are two ways of merging tables in SAS: SQL procedure and DATA step. SQL procedure provides a more thorough and transparent treatment of merging tables than DATA step. So we will discuss SQL procedure first.

SQL procedure can join two or more tables. Before discussing the coding details, we need to understand three basic join rules in SQL procedure: left join, full join, and join by a comma. First, how do SQL join two tables? It first creates a table as a Cartesian product. The Cartesian product means adding the first line of the first table to each line of the second table, and then adding the second line of the first table to each line of the second table, and so on and so forth. If the first table has m observations, and the second table has n observations, the Cartesian table of these two tables have m times n observations. After creating the Cartesian table, depending on the join type and conditions, SQL decides which observations in the Cartesian product table to keep and which observations to discard. Specifically, left join keeps all the observations of the left table no matter there is a match from right table or not. Full join keeps all the observations of both the left and right tables, matched or unmatched. Join by a comma is actually the Cartesian product itself. When join by a comma is coupled by a condition, only matched observations will be kept.

The following codes illustrate the differences of the three JOIN types.

```
data work.ab;
    a =1; b =2; output;
    a =2; b =3; output;
run;
data work.ac;
    a =2; c =3; output;
    a =3; c =4; output;
```

```
run;
proc sql;
  create table work.d as
  select a.*, b.c
  from work.ab as a left join work.ac as b
  on a.a = b.a
  order by a.a;

  create table work.e as
  select a.*, b.c
  from work.ab as a full join work.ac as b
  on a.a = b.a
  order by a.a;

  create table work.f as
  select a.*, b.c
  from work.ab as a, work.ac as b
  where a.a = b.a
  order by a.a;

  create table work.g as
  select a.*, b.c
  from work.ab as a, work.ac as b
  order by a.a;
quit;
```

Notice the following. First, the structure of the JOIN codes is FROM tables + Conditions. The left join and full join statements can only join two tables, whereas the join by a comma statement can join as many tables as we put in the codes. Second, the left join and full join statements require condition, whereas the condition is optional in the join by a comma statement. If no option is present in join by a comma statement, we get the Cartesian product table. If the condition is present in join by a comma statement, we get the matched observations from the Cartesian table. Compare work.f and work.g, we can understand the difference. Third, when the condition comprises of multiple components, use AND or OR to combine the components. Fourth, each of the tables to be joined are assigned an alias by AS statement. The purpose of the alias is to identify the tables. Why do we need identify the tables? That is because the SELECT statement and the condition refer to variables, and often times, the tables to be joined have same variables. Then we need to unambiguously tell SAS which table the variables come from. For example, table work. daily_mkt_idx contains the level of one stock market index over a series of days. We want to compute the 7-day returns on each day. The following codes can do the trick.

```
proc sql;
    create table work.weekly_ret_idx as
    select a.date as end_date, a.prc/b.prc-1 as ret
    from work.daily_mkt_idx as a left join work.daily_mkt_idx as b
    on a.date-7 = b.date
    order by a.date;
quit;
```

Given that there is the left join statement in SQL procedure, right join statement is also available, and it is just the mirror image of the left join statement.

3.3 Merging Tables in DATA Step Using MERGE Statement

In DATA step, we can use MERGE statement to merge two or more tables. There are two types of merge: one-to-one merge and match. With match merge, we use BY statement. We merge data sets using the MERGE statement in a DATA step. The form of the MERGE statement is the following:

```
MERGE SAS-data-set-list;
BY variable-list;
```

where SAS-data-set-list is the names of two or more SAS data sets to merge. The list may contain any number of data sets. Variable-list is one or more variables by which to merge the data sets. If we use a BY statement, then the data sets must be sorted by the same BY variables before we can merge them.

The difference between MERGE and concatenate can be summarized as follows. One visual difference is that the new data set gets wider after merging, while it gets longer after concatenating. After merging, the number of observations equals to that number in the largest data set. After concatenating, the number of observations equals to the total of all these numbers in the data sets.

Now let us look at match MERGE. Before match merging, make sure all the data sets have been sorted by the BY variable, using the following code:

```
proc sort data = company;
  by Name;
run;
```

Before match merging, the data sets must share a common variable. If we want the common variables in different data sets all appear in the final merged data set, then the RENAME statement should be used. The following is a simple example of match merging:

```
data repertory_name;
  merge finance repertory;
  by IdNumber;
run;
```

The following code drops some variables during merging. Note that when SAS processes the code, it first constructs a program data vector that contains all the variables, except those being excluded by the DROP statement, from all the data sets. Thus, dropping irrelevant variables within MERGE statement is more efficient.

```
data newrep (drop = IdNumber);
  merge finance (drop = Salary) repertory;
  by IdNumber;
run;
```

3.4 Modifying Tables

The Modify step firstly reads an observation from transaction dataset, then find a matched observation in master dataset. If there is no matched observation in master data set, SAS deems it an error. To prevent this, use the following codes:

```
If _iorc_ = 0 then replace; else _error_ = 0;
```

The first part instructs SAS that only the matched observations are updated; while the second part prevents SAS deem a failure of match as an error. To choose/alter/remove observation in the master data set according to the values of a variable in transaction data set, use the following codes:

```
    data master-dataset out-dataset; set transaction-
dataset;
      do until(_iorc_=%sysrc(_dsenom));
        modify master-dataset key=key-var;
        select (_iorc_);
          when (%sysrc(_sok)) do; if _iorc_=0 then …; end;
          when (%sysrc(_dsenom)) do; _error_=0; end;
          otherwise;
        end;
      end;
    run;
```

There are several issues worth mentioning. Firstly, the out-dataset can be omitted in the above codes if we modify the master data set only. Secondly, make sure both the master and the transaction data set have been assigned index of the key variable. But sorting according to the key variable is not required. Thirdly, make sure the transaction data set has no duplicate observations according to the key variable. Fourthly, replace means alter; output means output to the data set; remove means delete the observations. Attention should be paid to the output statement. If we write "output master-dataset", then the observation will be appended to the end of the master data set, which means the master data set will have multiple of this observation.

If we are to update the values of master data's several variables, notice the following. First, these variables do not need to be created beforehand. Second, the data have to be put into a new data set, rather than the master data set. Third, the undesired variables should be drop in the SET option. Fourth, notice that observations not present in the transaction data set will not be updated or output. So we should be very careful to think about what observations will remain.

Now let us look at how to modify a master data set with observations from a transaction data set. The syntax for using the MODIFY statement and the BY statement is

```
MODIFY master-SAS-data-set transaction-SAS-data-set;
BY by-variable;
```

When we use a BY statement with the MODIFY statement, the DATA step uses dynamic WHERE processing to find observations in the master data set. Neither the master data set nor the transaction data set needs to be sorted. For large data sets, however, sorting the data before we modify it can enhance performance significantly.

3.5 Transposing Tables

The following codes transpose a data set:

```
proc transpose
    data=work.j0223tp3 out=work.j0223tp4 (drop=_name__label_) prefix=Yr;
    by min &var;
    id bid_sig;
    var n;
run;
```

BY variables are the variables in the left columns, which are not changed.

Whenever the BY option is used, check if the data have been sorted according to the BY variable.

ID is the variable showed in the header of the right part of the transposed table. For example, ID option may assign variable Year. Then the right part of the table shows columns like 1990, 1991, 1992, ... If we want to add a prefix to each year, then use prefix option. That is, prefix = Yr. Then the right part of the headers become Yr1990, Yr1991, Yr1992, etc. Sometimes there're two columns in the original datasets, say the student ID and student name. If we specify ID student id, and we want the right part of the headers show student name, then we can add IDLABLE student name.

Option VAR specifies the variables that need to be transposed. Don't ignore this option. If it is ignored only numerical variables will be transposed, and there are no left column indicating what variables each rows are.

3.6 Subsetting Tables

We can use either WHERE or IF to subset a data set. The WHERE statement acts on the input data sets specified in the SET statement before observations are processed by the DATA step program, whereas the IF statement is executed as part of the DATA step program. If the input data set is indexed, using the WHERE statement can be more efficient than using the IF statement. However, the WHERE statement can only refer to variables in the input data set, not to variables computed by the DATA step program.

4

SAS Macros

In financial research, we often process the same data repeatedly or slightly change parameters when repeating the process that we have done before. In these scenarios, SAS macros can dramatically enhance efficiency.

4.1 Understanding the Basics of SAS Macros

When a macro facility is invoked, two steps happen successively. First, Macro facility compiles the macro, which results in a bulk of SAS codes. Second, these generated SAS codes are submitted. The first step is called compilation, while the second execution. In general, macro is a text generator. In compilation step, SAS tries as much as possible to resolve all the macro variables. Unless masked by quoting functions, special characters in the macro are treated as part of macro language, instead of the text to be generated. It should be made clear that macro language is not the same as SAS language. By SAS language, we mean the SAS codes to be submitted and run. Whereas macro language is what we use to construct the macro, and this macro then generates SAS language to run.

When writing SAS macros, we need to be very careful in choosing quoting functions. First, if the language does not contain special characters, no quoting functions are needed. Furthermore, if the language does contain special characters, we then check whether such special characters give rise to ambiguity. If no ambiguity incurs, no quoting functions are not needed either. For example, no quoting functions are needed between %DO and %END, because SAS does not expect any special characters between these two statements. In this case, any special characters contained between %DO and %END will be treated as part of text.

A macro definition is placed between a %MACRO statement and a %MEND (macro end) statement, as follows:

```
% MACRO macro-name;
macro definition
% MEND macro-name;
```

Here is a simple macro definition:

```
% macro dsn;
   Newdata
% mend dsn;
```

To call (or invoke) a macro, precede the name of the macro with a percent sign (%), as follows:

```
% macro-name
```

Although the call to the macro looks somewhat like a SAS statement, it does not have to end in a semicolon. For example, here is how we might call the DSN macro:

```
title "Display of Data Set % dsn";
```

Note that the title is enclosed in double quotation marks. In quoted strings in open code, the macro processor resolves macro invocations within double quotation marks but not within single quotation marks.

4.2 How SAS Executes a Macro

A macro variable defined in parentheses in a %MACRO statement is a macro parameter. Macro parameters enable we to pass information into a macro. Here is a simple example:

```
% macro plot(yvar = , xvar = );
    proc plot;
        plot &yvar * &xvar;
    run;
% mend plot;
```

We invoke the macro by providing values for the parameters, as follows:

```
% plot(yvar = income, xvar = age)
% plot(yvar = income, xvar = yrs_educ)
```

When the macro executes, the macro processor matches the values specified in the macro call to the parameters in the macro definition. (This type of parameter is called a keyword parameter.)

Macro execution produces the following code:

```
proc plot;
    plot income * age;
```

```
run;
proc plot;
  plot income*yrs_educ;
run;
```

To resolve a macro variable reference that occurs within a literal string, enclose the string in double quotation marks. Macro variable references that are enclosed in single quotation marks are not resolved. Compare the following statements that assign a value to macro variable DSN and use it in a TITLE statement:

```
%let dsn=Newdata;
title1 "Contents of Data Set &dsn";
title2 'Contents of Data Set &dsn';
```

In the first TITLE statement, the macro processor resolves the reference by replacing &DSN with the value of macro variable DSN. In the second TITLE statement, the value for DSN does not replace &DSN. SAS sees the following statements:

```
TITLE1 "Contents of Data Set Newdata";
TITLE2 'Contents of Data Set &dsn';
```

When we use an indirect macro variable reference, we must force the macro processor to scan the macro variable reference more than once and resolve the desired reference on the second, or the later scan. To force the macro processor to rescan a macro variable reference, we use more than one ampersand in the macro variable reference. When the macro processor encounters multiple ampersands, its basic action is to resolve two ampersands to one ampersand. For example, to append the value of &N to CITY and then reference the appropriate variable name, we use:

```
%put &&city&n; /* correct */
```

Assuming that &N contains 6, when the macro processor receives this statement, it performs the following steps:

resolves && to &

passes CITY as text

resolves &N into 6

Returns to the beginning of the macro variable reference, &CITY6, starts resolving from the beginning again, and prints the value of CITY6.

Using intnx function in macros can be tricky. Let us look at the following example:

`%let mnth = %sysfunc(intnx(month,'31jan1990'd,%eval(12*(&year-1990)+&mth-1),end));`

Notice that the parameters month and end in the intnx function do not use quotation marks, whereas the date 31jan1990 does use the quotation marks. Moreover, the calculation of the macro variables must be compounded in the % eval.

4.3 The Coding Rules in Macros That are Different From Other SAS Codes

If the special characters are contained in constants, then use %STR or %NRSTR. The latter is almost an alternate to the former, except that %NRSTR masks & and % while %STR cannot. In macro if we write nth = &I then, it's very likely that the nth variable is stored as a character, rather than numeric type. Also notice that we can change the type of a variable, which means we have to create a new variable to change the type of the current variable.

Macro quoting functions tell the macro processor to interpret special characters and mnemonics as text rather than as part of the macro language.

%let print = proc print; run;

In the above code, the macro processor will interpret the macro variable print as proc print. Notice that there is a blank after interpretion.

NR functions prevent macro and macro resolution. (NR means Not Resolved)

B functions are useful for unmatched quotation marks and parentheses. (B means By Itself)

%str %nrstr are compilation functions, which interpret special characters as text in a macro program statement.

%bquote %nrbquote are execution functions, which treat the special characters result from macro resolution as text.

Macro Quoting Function are only needed when we want the special characters to be part of the text, rather than part of the macro language. For example, in the following codes:

%do %until (&a = &b); --More SAS Codes; -- %end;

The = should be part of the macro language, so it does not need to be masked by macro quoting functions. Whereas in the following codes:

%do count = 1 % to &a; rename &var_old = &var_new; %end;

The = should be part of the text, so it needs to be masked.

The special characters, such as blanks, commas, etc, do not need to be masked. Because the macro facility does not expect any special characters between %do; and %end; there is no ambiguity, therefore no need to mask.

4.4 Return The Total Number of Observations

The following codes assign the value of the total number of observations to a macro variable "obs_of_dataset" which is defined in the 2nd line.

```
%let dsid = %sysfunc(open(%bquote(&DatasetFullName)));
%let obs_of_dataset = %sysfunc(attrn(&dsid, nobs));
%let rc = %sysfunc(close(&dsid));
```

The first line of codes defines which dataset to calculate the number of observations. The second line of codes uses the system function ATTRN to return the number of observations. The third line closes the data set opened in the first two lines.

Or use the following codes in a macro.

```
Data _null_; set mydata nobs = nobs; call symput ('n', nobs); run;
```

Another way to verify the data set REALLY exists is to use the following codes.

```
%macro x;
proc datasets
   library = work nolist;
   delete  libcont;
run;quit;


proc datasets library = temp MEMTYPE = all nolist;
   contents data = _all_ NODETAILS out = work.libcont
(keep = MEMNAME NOBS);
   run;quit;
%let valid_q = %str(No data return);
%let valid_t = %str(No data return);
data  work.libcont;
   set work.libcont;
```

```
       if MEMNAME = 'CQ' and NOBS >1 then call symput ('valid_
q', NOBS);
       if MEMNAME = 'CT' and NOBS >1 then call symput ('valid_
t', NOBS);
    run;
    % put valid_q &valid_q;
    % put valid_t &valid_t;
    % mend  x; % x;
```

The above macro tests if temp. cq and temp. ct really exists. It creates two macro variable, no matter the files exist or not. The macro variable & valid_q equals to the number of observations if temp. cq really exists, and if the file doesn't exist, it has the value of "No data return".

4.5 Existence of A Macro Variable and The Zero Observation of A Dataset

Use the following code to test if a macro variable, say &macvar, exists:

```
% if % symexist(macvar) % then % put EXISTS.;
```

Notice that the parameter of the % SYMEXIST function does not include the marco indicator &. We can use the % SYMEXIST function to test whether a dataset, say work. x, has any observations.

```
    data work.x1;
      set work.x0(where = (x >1));
      call symput ('n',_n_);
    run;
    % if % symexist(n) % then % put &n; % else % put 0 obs;
```

However, if the macro variable &n has been defined prior to the test, for example, % let n = 123. Then, the above code does not alter the value of &n, and % put &n still shows 123. To avoid such incidence, use the following:

```
% let n = 0;
data work.x1;
   set work.x0(where = (x >1));
   call symput ('n',_n_);
run;
% put &n;
```

5 Using SAS to Execute Financial Research Methodologies

5.1 Storing Results Generate by SAS Procedures

SAS has numerous procedures that we can use to process the data. For example, we can use the MEANS procedure to compute descriptive statistics for variables across all observations and within groups of observations. We can use the UNIVARIATE procedure to produce information on the distribution of numeric variables. Many other procedures are available through SAS. Often the time, the SAS procedure produces quite a few tables and charts in the output window. The question that many SAS users are asking is: How can we get these tables without just copying them from the output window? What if there are a huge number of such tables which makes copying too time consuming to be feasible? What if we need the output tables to be further processed in our SAS codes? The answer to these questions is simple. For virtually every table we see in the output window, we can always use ODS statements to export them to SAS data sets.

The key is to find the correct ODS table names. Apparently, for different procedures, the ODS table names are different. Therefore, readers need to check the SAS procedure manuals to get the names. Specifically, the SAS manual of each procedure contains a section called "ODS Table Names". The following codes provide an example of how to export some tables from REG procedure. It generates four tables of ANOVA, correlation matrix, residual statistics, and fit statistics, respectively. It should be noted that some of the ODS tables are generated by the procedure by default, whereas other ODS tables require specific statements of the procedure.

```
ods output
    ANOVA = work.output1
    Corr = work.output2
    ResidualStatistics = work.output3
    FitStatistics = work.output4;
proc reg ... ;
```

5.2   Summarizing Data and Statistical Tests

Understanding the data that we are dealing with is a vital, yet often overlooked step in the data analyses. The following codes help us understand the distributions of the data.

First, summarizing a data distribution. Notice that we cannot assign more than one variable after the VAR statement. That is, the above code generates a data set consisting of only one observation. If a CLASS OR BY statement is included, then the output data set will consist of multiple observations, like the following:

```
proc univariate data = rmf2.canton2;
by worker; var percentage; output out = work.abc2 mean = Mean nobs = NOBS STD = StandardDeviation VAR = Variance Max = MAX MIN = MIN KURTOSIS = KURTOSIS;
run; quit;
```

To generate histogram and test for a specific distribution, use the following codes:

```
proc univariate data = rmf2.canton2; by pocket; histogram percentage /normal; run;
```

Notice that we can also use CLASS statement instead of BY statement. If BY statement is used, the data set must be sorted according to the BY variable before. Another way of generating histogram can be found using PROC GCHART.

Statistical tests are the basic tools in data analyses. The following codes show how to conduct these tests. TTEST procedure is dedicated to conduct t tests. There are two types of t tests, i. e., testing whether the mean of the data is significantly different from a certain value, and testing whether the means of two or more than two groups of data are significantly different. Of course, we need to keep in mind that TTEST assumes the data under investigations follow normal distributions.

When we conduct the first type of the TTEST. The structure of the data is simple. We need only one variable, which is specified by the VAR statement. The following codes test if the students' scores are on average above 60.

```
ods output statistics = work.x1 ttests = work.x2;
proc ttest data = work.students_scores h0 = 60;
   var score;
   by course;
run;
```

The H0 statement in the above codes specifies the null hypothesis. In many statistical tests, when the null hypothesis is not explicitly expressed, it is often assumed to be 0. In other words, we are testing if the variable is significantly different from 0. Notice the BY statement in the above codes. We add this statement in order to test the mean scores of each course. If our data contain only one course, and we intend to test the scores of this course, then this BY statement should be omitted.

When we compare means of different groups, we need at least two columns in the data. One column specifies the CLASS variable, the other column specifies the variable that is going to be compared. For example, if we want to compare the scores of male and female students, the CLASS variable might be called gender, and the VAR variable might be called score. Also notice that the CLASS variable can have more than two values. In other words, TTEST procedure is able to compare more than two groups. BY statement instructs SAS to conduct TTEST for each group of BY variables. The following codes test if for each course the mean scores of the male students are significantly different from those of the female students.

```
ods output statistics = work.x1 ttests = work.x2;
proc ttest data = work.students_scores;
   class gender;
   var score;
   by course;
```

```
run;
```

When doing statistical tests, it is often necessary to compute significance levels. For a student t distribution, use the following (assuming two-tailed):

```
p = (1-probt(abs(t_statistics),df))*2;
```

As student t distribution approaches the normal distribution when the sample size is large, we can also use the following:

```
p = (1-probnorm(abs(t_statistics)))*2;
```

But in most cases, we may be interested with one-tail. So do not multiple 2.

Constructing portfolios is a widely used methodology in financial research. We can use procedure RANK to construct portfolios.

```
proc rank descending data = work.overall out = work.overall groups =10;
    var AvgReturn AvgExReturn;
    ranks AvgReturnRk AvgExReturnRk;
run;
```

If "descending" is added, the order is from the largest to the smallest. For example, a = 1, 2, 3, 4. Applying descending rank to variable a, then 1 has the largest group number, and 4 has the smallest group number. When the output dataset is the same as the input dataset, the codes simply add rank variables to the input dataset. If there's no by-group, then the RANK procedure does not require pre-sorting. If there's by-group, then the input dataset must be sorted by the by variables before being applied to the RANK procedure.

5.3 Regressions

Regression is arguably the most often used method in financial research. The following codes show how to conduct a simple OLS regression.

```
proc reg
data = work.tscomparison3 outest = work.tscomparison4
noprint EDF tableout;
    by Period MARank3;
    Fama3: model ExReturn = ExMarketReturn smb hml;
    Fama4: model ExReturn = ExMarketReturn smb hml mom;
run;quit;
```

To export estimated parameters, use OUTEST option in the PROC REG statement. To export fitted values, use OUTPUT OUT = option after the PROC REG statement.

For example, the following codes export the estimation to the data set rmf 2.P1Q2. To report R-square in the exported data set, use EDF option. To report Adjusted R-square, use/ADJRSQ in the MODEL statement. To report heteroscedasticity-consistent standard errors and t-statistics, use /HCC in the MODEL statement.

```
proc reg data = rmf2.anscombe noprint outest = rmf2.
P1Q2 tableout EDF;
    model y1 y2 y3 = x123 /ADJRSQ;
run; quit;
```

The following codes export the standardized and studentized residuals to data set work.abc. Notice that the statistics keywords must be supplied, otherwise SAS will generate error messages.

```
proc reg data = rmf2.anscombe noprint;
    model y1 = x123;
    output out = work.abc student = StandarizedResiduals
    rstudent = StudentizedResiduals;
```

```
run;quit;
```

Regression methods also involve the diagnostic analysis. Generally speaking, what concerns us is the validation of assumptions underlying linear regression. To this end, we conduct diagnostic analysis of the regression. There are several things we want to test: 1) the independence of error terms with dependent, independent, and fitted variables, 2) the homoscedasticity of error terms, 3) the normality of error terms. The first two are about the validity of using linear regression. The third is about the accuracy of predictions.

The most mostly frequently used methods to test for the first two assumptions is to plot residuals against dependent variable, independent variables, and fitted values. Notice that we have three types of residuals. The original residuals, the standardized residuals, and the studentized residuals, whose statistics keywords in SAS are RESIDUALS. , STUDENT. , RSTUDENT. , respectively. To plot the residuals against the above three variables, use the following codes:

```
proc reg data = rmf2.anscombe;
 model y1 = x123;
 plot  residual.*predicted.
   student.*predicted.
   rstudent.*predicted.
   residual.*y1;
   residual.*x123;
run;
```

To test for the error terms' normality, first save the residuals, then fit the residuals using PROC UNIVARIATE.

Panel regressions pose more restrictions on the assumptions of the data, therefore new methods are needed (see Petersen (2009), Hjalmarsson (2011), and Thompson (2011) for more detailed discussions). In glm or genmod, the

CLASS option generates dummies, and to let these dummies really incorporated in the regression, the CLASS variable should also in the regression. If we want to control cluster, we can use REPEATED option in GENMOD procedure. And the cluster variable should also appear following CLASS option, although it may not need to appear in the MODEL option.

A fixed effects regression using the absorption technique can be done as follows:

```
Proc  glm;
    absorb  firm;
    class  time;
    model  depvar = indvars  time/solution; run;
quit;
```

The above regression controls the firm and time effects. Notice time also appears in model options, but firm doesn't appear. The following codes give the same results as the above codes.

```
Proc  glm;
    class  time firm;
    model  depvar = indvars time firm/solution; run;
quit;
```

Notice now we have both time and firm appear in the model options. The parameter estimates are the same. The former is faster but no results on firm dummies are reported. The latter is slower and reports results for both firm and time dummies. The reason is that the former uses the deviation from firm means, while the latter uses traditional firm dummies.

Running a Fama-MacBeth (Fama and MacBeth (1973)) regression is another panel regression method. It doesn't require any special macros. The following code will run cross-sectional regressions by year for all firms and report

the means:
```
ods  listing  close;
ods  output   parameterestimates=pe;
proc reg
  data=dset;
  by   year;
  model depvar=indvars;
run; quit;
ods listing;
proc means
  data  =pe mean std t probt;
  var   estimate;
  class variable;
run;
```
Since the results from this approach give a time-series, it is common practice to use the Newey-West adjustment for standard errors. The approach here is to use GMM to regress the time-series estimates on a constant, which is equivalent to taking a mean. This works because the Newey-West adjustment gives the same variance as the GMM procedure.

5.4 Simulation Methods

Simulations are powerful statistical tools. Often the time, the executions of simulations are highly case-specific, which means we need to write the codes to do every step of the simulations. A vital building block of codes for simulations is to generate random numbers, although mathematically any series of numbers generated by a deterministic function are not really random. It is important to keep in mind that the so-called random numbers generated by SAS is generated by functions which in turn depend on the "seeds". The "seeds" are the numbers that we initially feed to the function in order to start generating random numbers. Although seeds are not compulsory in the function, it is a good practice to always explicitly assign the seeds. That is because we will get a different series of random numbers, and hence probably slightly different results, every time we ran the same SAS codes, if we do not assign the seeds and effectively leave the assigning job to SAS.

The simplest way to generating random numbers is shown in the following codes:

```
data work.generated;
  call streaminit(1234);
  do i =1 to 1000;
    x1 = rand('Normal');
    x2 = rand('Normal', 1,10);
    x3 = rand('Uniform');
    output;
  end;
run;
```

In the above codes, "call streaminit (1234)" sets the seeds. This line of codes guarantees the same results every time we run the codes, unless the seed, which is 1234 in this case, is changed. The above codes generate three series of random numbers. X1 series follow the standard normal distribution. X2 series follow a normal distribution with a mean of 1 and a standard deviation of 10. X3 series follow a uniform distribution over the range of 0 to 1.

To get random numbers that follow other distributions, we can change the parameter in the RAND function. For example, parameters BETA, F, and GAMMA generate random numbers that follow beta distribution, F distribution, and gamma distribution, respectively.

Surely SAS provides other functions to generate random numbers. For example, function RANNOR generates random numbers that follows a standard-normal distribution. However, function RAND is recommended because of both its efficiency and versatility.

Among function RAND's parameters of distribution names, there is a special one "Table". Take a look at the following example. Assume that we have roster of 100 students. Each of the students enrolls in one and only one of the three different classes, e. g. , corporate finance class, asset pricing class, and financial engineering class. Further assume that 50% of the students enroll in the corporate finance class, 30% of the students enroll in the asset pricing class, and 20% of the students enroll in the financial engineering class. The following codes assumes that the students are recorded according to the variable i, and are randomly assigned to one of each class according to the probability of each class. The assignment is shown in three dummy variables: p1, p2, and p3, corresponding to the corporate finance class, asset pricing class, and financial engineering class. For example, if SAS assigns a student to the corporate finance class, this student's p1 will be 1, while his or her p2 and p3 will be 0.

```
data work.rand_table;
  call streaminit (1234);
  array p[3] (0.5 0.3 0.2);
  do i =1 to 100;
    student_class = rand('Table', of p[ * ]);
    output;
```

```
    end;
run;
```

Notice the above codes, the code "array p [n] (x1 x2...xn);" defines the probabilities of the three classes. The probabilities need to sum to 1. Then RNAD function generates the random numbers that following the "Table" distribution.

We can also use the Table distribution to combine different distributions in order to generate a series of random numbers that come from "no distribution". This function is very useful in simulations given that it is often wise to assume no specific distribution instead of a specific one. The logic is as follows. Each time the code generates a random number, the parameters of the generating distribution is also randomly determined by SAS. The following codes provide an example:

```
data work.rand_table2;
    call streaminit (1234);
    array p[3] (0.5 0.3 0.2);
    do i = 1 to 1000;
        from_dist_type = rand('Table', of p[ * ]);
        if from_dist_type = 1 then x = rand('Normal',3,1);
        else if from_dist_type = 2 then x = rand('Normal',8,2);
        else if from_dist_type = 3 then x = rand('Normal',10,3);
        output;
    end;
run;
```

Bootstrapping is another simulation method in finance research. It creates random samples from the existing sample. To be more accurate, it just randomly chooses observations from the existing sample and repeats this choosing from a lot of times. The following codes show how to use SAS to generate a bootstrapping sample.

```
proc surveyselect data = work.sample_data out = work.
out_data seed = 1234 method = urs sampsize = 1 rep = 1000
outhits noprint;
    strata stkcd;
run;
```

In the above codes, work. sample_ data is the existing sample, and work. out_ data is the output sample. There are three statements in SURVEYSELECT procedure to determine how to randomly choose observations from the existing sample every time, i. e., method, sampsize, and strata. "method = urs" instructs SAS to choose observations with replacement. If we need to choose without replacement, we can specify method = srs. The sampsize statement specifies how many observations SAS choose from the existing sample every time. Strata statements are similar to the BY statement in many other SAS codes. If Strata statement is used, SAS will choose observations from each of the group specified by the variables in the Strata statement. If Strata statement is omitted, SAS will choose from the whole sample. The Rep statement specifies how many times SAS chooses from the existing sample.

5.5 Event Studies

Event study is a methodology that is widely used in financial research. The basic idea of event study is to decompose a stock's return into two parts: the expected return and the abnormal return. The expected return refers to the stock return predicted by an asset pricing model. The actual return minus the expected return is the abnormal return. Given that the asset pricing literature has shown strong evidence that market return is the most important factor of stock return, the price changes of a stock are largely driven by the market movement. If we are trying to show that certain news causes a stock's price to drop, it is more suitable to use the abnormal return rather than the actual return. That is because if the market goes higher, it is more likely the stock price also goes up, generating a positive rather than negative return. MacKinlay (1997) provides a detailed discussion on how to calculate the standard errors in an event study. Kolari and Pynnönen (2010) also cover this topic. The following codes define a SAS macro to conduct event studies:

```
% macro event_study (eventlistdata = ,
dailyretdata = ,
mktretdata = none,
ar_data = ,
detailed_ar_data = ,
stkidvar = ,
eventdtIDvar = ,
dailyretvar = ,
mktretvar = ,
group_var = none,
esti_s = ,
esti_e = ,
evt_s = ,
evt_e = ,
del_unwanted = yes
)/store;
```

5 Using SAS to Execute Financial Research Methodologies

```
proc sql;
   create table work.esti_window0 as
   select a.eventno, b.&dailyretvar*1 as ret,
      % if &mktretdata = none % then % do; b.&mktretvar*1
as mktret % end;
      % else % do; b.date % end;
   from &eventlistdata ( keep = eventno &stkidvar
&eventdtIDvar) as a,
        &dailyretdata (keep = &stkidvar date dtID ret % if
&mktretdata = none % then % do; &mktretvar % end;) as b
   where a.&stkidvar = b.&stkidvar and a.&eventdtIDvar-
&esti_s < = b.dtID < = a.&eventdtIDvar-&esti_e
   order by a.eventno;
quit;

% if &mktretdata ne none % then % do;
proc sql;
   create table work.esti_window0 as
   select a.*, b.&mktretvar*1 as mktret
   from work.esti_window0 as a, &mktretdata as b
   where a.date = b.date
   order by a.eventno;
quit;
% end;

data work.esti_window1 (keep = eventno n);
   set work.esti_window0 (where = (ret*mktret ne .));
```

```
   by eventno;
   if first.eventno then n =1;
   else n +1;
   if last.eventno and n > = 15 and n > = 0.8 * ( &esti_s -
&esti_e);
   run;
  proc sql;
   create table work.esti_window2 as
   select a.*
   from work.esti_window0 (where = (ret * mktret ne .))
as a, work.esti_window1 as b
   where a.eventno = b.eventno
   order by a.eventno;
  quit;


  ods listing close; ods html close; run;quit;
  ods output FitStatistics = work.fit ( keep = eventno
nvalue1 label1 where = (Label1 in ('Root MSE',' 均方根误差')));
   proc reg data = work.esti_window2 outest = work.est
(keep = eventno intercept mktret _type_ where = ( _type_ =
'PARMS')) edf tableout plots = none;
    model ret = mktret;
    by eventno;
  run;quit;
  ods listing;


  data work.alpha_beta (drop = label1 _type_ rename =
```

```
(intercept = alpha mktret = beta nvalue1 = rmse));
     merge work.fit work.est;
     by eventno;
     attrib _all_ label = '';
   run;

   proc sql;
     create table work.event_window0 as
     select b.*, a.&eventdtIDvar, a.&stkidvar % if &group
_var ne none % then % do; ,a.&group_var % end;
     from &eventlistdata as a, work.alpha_beta as b
     where a.eventno = b.eventno;

     create table work.event_window1 as
     select a.eventno, a.rmse, b.dtID-a.&eventdtIDvar as
T, b.&dailyretvar-a.alpha-a.beta*c.&mktretvar as AR
        % if &group_var ne none % then % do; ,a.&group_var
% end;
     from work.event_window0 as a, &dailyretdata as b,
&mktretdata as c
     where a.&stkidvar = b.&stkidvar and b.date = c.date
and a.&eventdtIDvar + &evt_s < = b.dtID < = a.&eventdtIDvar
+ &evt_e
     order by a.eventno, b.dtID;
   quit;

   data &detailed_ar_data (drop = _CAR _Variance);
```

```
    set work.event_window1;
    by eventno T;
    retain _CAR _variance;
    Variance_AR = rmse**2;
    Sigma_AR = rmse;
    tValue_AR = AR/rmse;
    if AR < =0 then pValue_AR = probnorm(tValue_AR);
    else pValue_AR =1-probnorm(tValue_AR);
    if first.eventno then do;
       CAR = AR; Variance_CAR = Variance_AR;
    end;
    else do;
       CAR = AR + _CAR; Variance_CAR = Variance_AR + _Variance;
    end;
    Sigma_CAR = sqrt(Variance_CAR);
    tValue_CAR = CAR/Sigma_CAR;
    if tValue_CAR < =0 then pValue_CAR = probnorm(tValue_CAR);
    else pValue_CAR =1-probnorm(tValue_CAR);
    output;
    _CAR = CAR;
    _Variance = Variance_CAR;
 run;

 proc sql;
    create table work.event_window2 as
```

```
    select 'CAR' as Type format = $3., % if &group_var ne
none % then % do; &group_var, % end; T,
        mean(CAR) as AbnormalReturn,
        sqrt (mean (Variance_CAR)/N (CAR)) as Sigma,
        mean (CAR)/(sqrt (mean (Variance_CAR)/N (CAR)))
as tValue,
        case
            when mean (CAR)/(sqrt (mean (Variance_CAR)/N
(CAR))) < 0 then probnorm (mean (CAR)/ (sqrt (mean
(Variance_CAR)/N (CAR))))
                else 1 - probnorm (mean (CAR)/ (sqrt (mean
(Variance_CAR)/N (CAR))))
        end as pValue
    from &detailed_ar_data
    group by % if &group_var ne none % then % do; &group_
var, % end; T
    order by % if &group_var ne none % then % do; &group_
var, % end; T;


    create table work.event_window3 as
    select 'AR' as Type format = $3., % if &group_var ne
none % then % do; &group_var, % end; T,
        mean (AR) as AbnormalReturn,
        sqrt (mean (Variance_AR)/N (AR)) as Sigma,
        mean (AR)/(sqrt (mean (Variance_AR)/N (AR)))
as tValue,
        case
```

```
            when mean(AR)/(sqrt(mean(Variance_AR)/N
(AR)))<0 then probnorm(mean(AR)/(sqrt(mean(Variance_
AR)/N(AR))))
                else 1-probnorm(mean(AR)/(sqrt(mean
(Variance_AR)/N(AR))))
            end as pValue
    from &detailed_ar_data
    group by %if &group_var ne none %then %do; &group_
var, %end; T
    order by %if &group_var ne none %then %do; &group_
var, %end; T;
    quit;

    data &ar_data;
      set work.event_window2 work.event_window3;
      if pValue<=0.01 then Significance='* * *';
      else if pValue<=0.05 then Significance='* *';
      else if pValue<=0.1 then Significance='*';
    run;
    data &ar_data;
      retain Type %if &group_var ne none %then %do;
&group_var %end; T AbnormalReturn Significance pValue;
      set &ar_data;
    run;

    %if &del_unwanted=yes %then %do;
    proc datasets library=work nolist;
```

```
   delete alpha_beta est esti_window0 esti_window1 esti_
window2 event_window0
                event _ window1  event _ window2  event _
window3 fit;
   run;quit;
   %end;


   %mend event_study;
```

6

Research on Mutual Funds

6.1 The Major Research Questions in Mutual Fund Studies

Mutual fund performance has been extensively studied during the past several decades. There are several patterns of fund performances. The following is a very brief review of the classic studies in this area.

The first issue is the persistence of fund performances. If fund performances are persistent, fund clients may choose a superior fund into which to put their money. In this sense, this question is of importance. Fund performances persistence is well documented, but not well explained, noted by Carhart (1997).

Fund performance persistence is also called "hot hand" phenomenon. That is, hot hand is a synonym of performance persistence. The researches supporting hot hand include: Hendricks, Patel and Zeckhauser (1993), Goetzmann and Ibbotson (1994), and Brown and Goetzmann (1995), which document the short-term performance persistence and attribute this to hot hand or investment strategy; Grinblatt and Titman (1992), Elton, Gruber and Blake (1996a) and Elton, Gruber and Blake (1996b), which document the long-term performance persistence and attribute this to fund manager's stock-picking talents.

Let us take a closer look at this question. If hot hand exists, then how long does it last? Short term or long term? When these questions are answered, fund clients can use performances as an indicator when choosing funds to invest in. If hot hand does not exist, fund clients can draw nothing informative when choosing funds. And it is bad news for both fund clients and fund managers. This question is closely related to the question I am very much interested in. Is fund industry worthy existing? If hot hand exists, the answer to this question is a strong yes. If it does not, the question is hard to answer. If fund managers happen to be lucky so that outperform markets, and if fund industry, as a whole, does not outperform markets, then the answer might be no. Oh, perhaps not. Fund industry provides a way for small investors to trade a portfolio of stocks with relatively small money. In this sense, even though funds by no means outperform, we need them after all.

The second issue is the fund manager's skills. In other words, this line of studies tries to understand if the fund managers as a whole or any individual managers can outperform the market. There are two approaches to evaluate fund manager's skills (Wermers, 2000): return-based and holding-based approaches. The holding-based approach investigates whether fund managers can pick out outperforming stocks. If they do, they are said to have skills. The critiques against fund manager's ability to beat the market come in the following ways. Firstly, they cannot outperform their passively managed counterparts. Secondly, the more they trade, the higher the transaction cost is, furthermore, the lower the return is. Notice this critique. It does not say that they should not trade, they just say their trade destroys rather than adds value. This critique is also proposed by Carhart (1997). Kosowski, Timmermann and Wermers *et al.* (2006) also argue for the existence of fund managers' superior ability. Grinblatt and Titman (1989), Grinblatt and Titman (1993), and Gibson, Safieddine and Sonti (2004) show weak evidence that fund managers add value.

The third issue is related how mutual funds invest. Most importantly–maybe a bit disappointingly – prior research found that mutual funds tend to herd. Scharfstein and Stein (1990) argue that managers will mimic the decisions of other managers. This herding behavior is rational in the views of managers. This herding behavior is due to manager's concern about their reputation in the labor market. That is, it hurts the manager's reputation to be "lone fools," and "there would be comfort in numbers" if things go wrong. In this setting, managers will pay more attention to what other managers do, instead of their own private signals. Of course, these happen in the market with asymmetric information on manager's skills. Zwiebel (1995) discuss similar ideas.

In Scharfstein *et al.* (1990) model, "managers who care only about their reputation will always herd… but managers who care about profits will have to trade off the loss of reputation against profits" (from Dass, Massa and Patgiri, 2008 Page 52). Dass *et al.* (2008) explore this trade off using the data around the 2000 market bubbles. They show that high incentive contract will induce managers invest less on bubble stocks, or put differently, will lead managers to less herding. Their findings cast new lights on the "limit of arbitrage" literature.

Other epirical evidence on mutual fund herding can be found in Wermers (1999), Grinblatt, Titman and Wermers (1995), Sias (2004).

As for the effect of institutional herding on the stock prices, the current empirical evidences are mixed. Dasgupta, Prat and Verardo (2011) comment: "Studies examining the short-term impact of institutional trading generally find that herding has a stabilizing effect on prices. In contrast, studies focusing on longer horizons often find that herding predicts reversals in returns, thus providing empirical evidence in favor of Trichet's view (that is, destabilizing the market) (page 1)."

Given the disappointing results that mutual fund industry as a whole tends to underperform the market, prior literature strives to understand what hinder these professional and dedicated money managers fail to create incremental values for fund investors compared to what the investors could get by simply putting their money in passive benchmark indices. Incentives of fund managers are found to be an important factor. One problem is to set the optimal contract. The other problem is how the contract affects investing.

When investigating the optimal contract, researchers are concerned with the agency costs borne by the investors. The optimal contract should entice the fund managers to choose optimal portfolio (and risk), and entice them to exert the best effort. Massa and Patgiri (2009) summary these two themes of optimal contract in the following way, although they do not intend to answer this theoretical question. "Agency theory claims that investors can alleviate some agency problems through high-incentive contracts for managers. Such contracts would mean that managers' payoffs were more closely related to their performance, which could increase managers' efforts and thus lead to better performance. At the same time, high-incentive contracts would also induce managers to take more risks. (page 1777)." The following studies discuss the optimal contract Dybvig,

Farnsworth and Carpenter (2010).

As for the effects of contract on fund performance, one line of inquiry discusses the risk-taking shift under specific contract. The other line investigates empirically: Which type of contract "generates" higher return? Both lines assume the contract as given. Non-linear performance-flow relationship is a call option in terms of fund manager's compensation (Sirri and Tufano, 1998). This relation affects fund manager's risk-taking behavior. See Chevalier and Ellison (1997), Brown, Harlow and Starks (1996), Busse (2001), Goriaev, Nijman and Werker (2005), Chen and Pennacchi (2009). These studies are "tournament" researches. Notice that fund managers may alter two kinds of riskiness of the fund's portfolios: standard deviation of the "track errors" and of the returns (Chen et al., 2009).

Massa et al. (2009) investigate empirically whether high-incentive funds deliver higher performance. Their motivation is that high-incentive, on one hand, align the interests of investors and managers better, on the other hand, it encourages managers to take more risks. They want to investigate which effect dominate. They find managers do take more risks, but they can deliver more superior performance.

Elton, Gruber and Blake (2003) study the incentive fees. The incentive fees scheme, to some extent, alter the incentives of the fund managers. With fixed fees, fund managers are encouraged to expand the size of fund under management. With incentive fees, fund managers are aligned with that of the investors.

What spoil the financial industry? By spoil, I mean the distorted incentive scheme, which results in aggressive risk-taking. The answer is simple, when the game is such that we have little to lose, while a lot to win, we are surely aggressive.

Brown et al. (1996) argue that fund industry is inherently of tournament nature. Thus interim losers will increase the risk level of his fund to try to fill the "deficit." Aware of what their interim loser competitors will do, interim winners will also increase the risk level, but to a lower extent. Furthermore, size and age negatively affect this risk level adjustment, which predicts that new funds and small funds will act more progressively when increasing risk level.

The last issue is about fund flow. Fund flow refers to the flow of fund investors. When the investors purchase a fund product, there is a flow into the fund. When the investors redeem a fund product, there is a flow out of the fund. There are two main research questions in this area. The first is whether the fund flow is smart, meaning whether an inflow can predict outperformance and an outflow can predict underperformance. The second question is whether fund flow affect fund performance.

Due to the non-linear performance-flow relationship, fund managers are granted a call option, in the sense if a remarkably high return is achieved, a large amount of funds will be poured into his fund; while if a modest or even poor return is achieved, relatively less funds will withdraw. Brown et al. (1996) and Chevalier et al. (1997) explicitly discussed this topic and have shown that fund managers increase the volatility of his fund to maximize the value of this call option, especially during the later part of the calendar year. Also see Ippolito (1992), Gruber (1996), Sirri et al. (1998), Goetzmann and Peles (1997), Del Guercio and Tkac (2002) for more discussions on this topic.

Lynch and Musto (2003) explicitly take into account the replacement of fund manager and stock-picking algorithm. Since investor's delegation of his money to fund implies delegation of choosing "right" fund manager and choosing "right" stock-picking algorithm, investors may reasonably expect that bad performing fund managers in the current period may be replaced by other fund manager, or they may choose a different stock-picking algorithm. So why bother withdrawing their money from the bad performing funds?

6.2 Calculating Fund Returns

To conduct mutual fund research, the first step is to calculate fund returns. Although many research database, such as CSMAR, have already compute the fund returns, the readily available return data may not be suitable for a specific research question. For example, the research database provides daily returns, weekly returns, monthly returns, etc. However, a specific research question may require a 15-day return. Thus, computing fund returns by ourselves is necessary work for our research. The following codes show how to compute the fund returns based on the original data provided in CSMAR.

```
/* ------------------------Open-end Fund Daily
-------------------------------- */
Data cnmarket.of_d;
   Set csmar.OF_Ofddntval;
   Date = clsdt;
   Week = intnx ( 'Week', intnx ('year', Date, 0, 'beginning'),
int ( (datdif (intnx ('year', Date, 0, 'beginning'), Date, 'act/
act') )/7 ), 'SameDay' );
   Month = intnx ( 'month', Date, 0, 'beginning' );
   Quarter = intnx ( 'quarter', Date, 0, 'end' );
   Semiyear = intnx ( 'semiyear', Date, 0, 'end' );
   Year = intnx ( 'year', Date, 0, 'end' );
   NetAssets = Accnav1;
```

```
        NominalNetAssets = Naps;
        Return = Accnrt1/100;
        format Date week month quarter semiyear year date9.;
    run;
    proc sql;
      create table cnmarket.of_d as
      select a.*,
         a.Return - b.RiskFreeReturn as ExReturn,
         b.RiskFreeReturn,
         b.LagRiskFreeReturn as LagRiskFree
      from cnmarket.of_d as a left join cnmarket.rf_d as b
      on a.Date = b.Date;

      create table cnmarket.of_d as
      select a.*,
         b.ValueWeighted as MarketReturn,
         b.ValueWeighted-a.RiskFreeReturn as ExMarketReturn,
         b.LagValueWeighted as LagMarketReturn,
         b.LagValueWeighted-a.LagRiskFree as LagEx
MarketReturn,
         b.SMB, b.HML, b.MOM
      from cnmarket.of_d as a left join cnmarket.market_d
as b
      on a.Date = b.Date
      order by a.fundcd, a.Date;
    quit;
    data cnmarket.of_d;
```

```
    set cnmarket.of_d;
    by fundcd Date;
    LagReturn = Lag ( Return );
    LagExReturn = LagReturn - LagRiskFree;
    if first.fundcd then do;
      LagReturn = .;
      LagExReturn = .;
    end;
run;

proc sql;
    alter table cnmarket.of_d
    drop MCONME, DEPNAME, FUNTYPE, INVTAR, ARGET, LISTTYPE,
LISTLOC, QDII, ConvertedClose, Estbdt;

    create table cnmarket.of_d as
    select a.*, b.MCONME, b.DEPNAME, b.FUNTYPE, b.INVTAR,
b.ARGET, b.LISTTYPE, b.LISTLOC, b.QDII, b.ConvertedClose,
b.Estbdt
    from cnmarket.of_d as a left join cnmarket.of_type as b
    on a.fundcd = b.fundcd and b.Begdt <= a.Date <= Enddt
    order by a.fundcd, a.Date;
quit;

/* -----------Test for Errors in cnmarket.of_d ----
------------------
data work.x;
```

```
    set cnmarket.of_d;
  if MCONME eq " or DEPNAME eq" or FUNTYPE eq " or INVTAR
eq" or "ARGET eq"
    or LISTTYPE eq . or LISTLOC eq . or QDII eq " or
ConvertedClose eq" or Estbdt eq.;
  run;
  proc sort data = work.x out = work.x1 nodupkey;
    by fundcd;
  run;
  proc sql;
    create table work.cn as
    select a.*
    from cnmarket.of_d as a, work.x1 as b
    where a.fundcd = b.fundcd
    order by a.fundcd, a.date;
    create table work.type as
    select a.*
    from work.fundstypes as a, work.x1 as b
    where a.fundcd = b.fundcd
    order by a.fundcd;
  quit;


       -----------Test for Errors in cnmarket.of_d ------
  ---------------- * /
    /* -----------Correct Errors in cnmarket.of_d -----
  ---------------- * /
      ...
```

```
/* ----------Correct Errors in cnmarket.of_d ----
----------------- */
```

6.3 Calculating Fund Alpha's Using a Macro

Once we have the fund return data, it is natural to calculate Fund's Alphas. Alpha can have different definitions. The following codes show how to calculate the classic CAPM Alphas, Fama–French 3 Factor Alphas, and Fama–French 4 Factor Alphas. Moreover, the following codes create a SAS macro in order to calculate the Alphas in different frequencies. As mentioned in the previous chapters, SAS macros are efficient tools for doing repetitive work.

```
/* Alpha and return standard deviation
All calculated using daily data, and the results are
converted to the qurarterly counterparts by multipling 60 */
% macro alpha (type = );
% stdm_timefrequency (type = &type) run;
% put n_trade is &n_trade;
proc means data  = cnmarket.of_d  noprint;
   output out = work.sum_&type  (drop = _type_ _freq_)
   N (ExReturn)  = Num  std (Return)  = Sigma;
   by  fundcd &type2;
run;
proc sql;
   create table  work.of_d  as
   select a.fundcd, a.&type2, a.Exreturn, a.Exmarketreturn,
        a.smb,  a.hml,  a.mom,  b.Num
```

```
        from   cnmarket.of_d   as   a,   work.sum_&type as   b
        where  a.fundcd   = b.fundcd   and   a.&type2 = b.&type2
        order  by  a.fundcd,  a.&type2;
    quit;


    proc  reg  data   = work.of_d (where = (num > 15))   noprint
outest = work.reg_&type   EDF tableout;
        CAPM: model ExReturn = ExMarketReturn; by fundcd &
type2;
          Fama3: model ExReturn = ExMarketReturn smb hml; by
fundcd &type2;
          Fama4: model ExReturn = ExMarketReturn smb hml mom; by
fundcd &type2;
      run;quit;


    proc  sql;
       create table  work.reg_&type as
         select   a.fundcd, a.&type2,
                  a. Intercept * &n _ trade     as     CAPM _ Alpha
format = percent8.4,
                  a.ExMarketReturn   as   CAPM_Beta,
                  b. Intercept * &n _ trade    as     Fama3 _ Alpha
format = percent8.4,
                  b.ExMarketReturn  as  Fama3_Beta,
                  c. Intercept * &n _ trade    as    Fama4 _ Alpha
format = percent8.4,
                  c.ExMarketReturn   as   Fama4_Beta
```

```
        from  work.reg_&type  as  a, work.reg_&type as b,
work.reg_&type as c
        where  a.fundcd = b.fundcd = c.fundcd and a.&type2 = b.
&type2 = c.&type2 and a._type_ = b._type_ = c._type_ = 'PARMS'
and a._model_ = 'CAPM' and b._model_ = 'Fama3' and c._model_ =
'Fama4';

        create table work.reg_&type as
        select a.fundcd, a.&type2,
            a.Sigma * &n_trade as Sigma format = percent8.4
Label = 'Sigma: Standard deviation of the daily return
during the period, converted to current frequency',
            b.CAPM_Alpha, b.CAPM_Beta, b.Fama3_Alpha, b.Fama3_
Beta, b.Fama4_Alpha, b.Fama4_Beta
        from   work.sum_&type as a left join work.reg_&type
as b
        on   a.fundcd = b.fundcd and a.&type2 = b.&type2
        order   by   a.fundcd, a.&type2;
    quit;

    proc  datasets  library  = work nolist;
        delete  reg_&type  sum_&type  of_d;
    run;quit;
    % mend alpha;
    % alpha (type = a)
    % alpha (type = s)
    % alpha (type = q)
```

6.4 Calculating Fund Flows

Fund flows are important research questions in the field. To conduct this research, we need to calculate the funds' total net asset (TNA) first. That is because the fund flow data are not published by fund management companies, and therefore can only be estimated by the change of the fund's TNA. The following codes show how to calculate the fund's TNA.

```
/* ------------------------- Quarterly -------
--------------------------------- */
/* Fund's flow data */
/* The most frequent data on fund share change is
quarterly, from csmar.OF_Ofundteyw */

/* Check the data of csmar.OF_Ofundteyw */
data work.x;
  set csmar.OF_Ofundteyw;
  date = cats( month(clsdt), '-', day(clsdt) );
run;
proc sort data = work.x out = work.x1 ( keep = date ) nodupkey;
  by date;
run;
/* Nonregular date: 4-28 */
data work.x1;
  set work.x;
```

```
    if date ='4-28';
run;
  * only one obs fundcd =020008;
data work.x1;
   set work.x;
   if fundcd ='020008';
run;
/* Nonregular date, solution: transform it into quarter */
data work.x (drop =clsdt date);
   set work.x (drop =old_clsdt);
   Quarter =intnx ( 'quarter', clsdt, 0, 'end' );
   format Quarter date9.;
run;


/* Duplicate reports */
proc sort data =work.x nodupkey;
   by fundcd quarter;
run;
/* No duplicate reports */
/* finish checking csmar.OF_Ofundteyw */
data work.sharechg;
   set work.x;
run;


data work.lastdayofquarter;
  set cnmarket. of _ d ( keep = fundcd quarter Date
```

```
NominalNetAssets NetAssets );
    by fundcd quarter Date;
    if first.fundcd or last.quarter;
run;
data work.lastdayofquarter;
  set work.lastdayofquarter;
  by fundcd quarter;
  LagNNA = Lag (NominalNetAssets);
  LagNA = Lag ( NetAssets );
    if not first.fundcd;
run;
data work.test;
   set work.lastdayofquarter;
   if Lagnna = . or NominalNetAssets = .;
run;


proc sql;
    alter table cnmarket.of_q ( alter = password write = password )
      drop TotalShares, LagTotalShares, AvgTotalShares, SharesChange,
        PctSharesChange, SharesIn, PctSharesIn, SharesOut, PctSharesOut,
        NetAssets, LagNetAssets, NominalNetAssets, LagNominalNetAssets,
        TNA, LagTNA, AvgTNA, CashInFlow, CashOutFlow, CashNetFlow, CashNetFlow2,
```

```
    PctCashInFlow, PctCashOutFlow, PctCashNetFlow;

    create table cnmarket.of_q ( alter = password write =
password ) as
    select a.*,
    b.Lafqut as TotalShares format = comma32. Label =
'TotalShares: Total Number of Shares at the End of
the Quarter',
    b.Eafqut as LagTotalShares format = comma32. Label =
'LagTotalShares: Total Number of Shares at the End of the
Previous Quarter',
    b. Exbqut as SharesIn format = comma32. Label =
'SharesIn: Number of Shares Inflow',
    b. Atoqut as SharesOut format = comma32. Label =
'SharesOut: Number of Shares Outflow'
    from cnmarket.of_q as a left join work.sharechg as b
    on a.fundcd = b.fundcd and a.quarter = b.quarter;


    create table cnmarket.of_q ( alter = password write =
password ) as
    select a.*,
    b.NetAssets Label = 'NetAssets: Adjusted Net Assets
Per Share at the end of the Quarter',
    b. LagNA as LagNetAssets Label = 'LagNetAssets:
Adjusted Net Assets Per Share at the end of previous
Quarter',
    b. NominalNetAssets Label = 'NominalNetAssets:
```

UnAdjusted Net Assets Per Share at the end of the Quarter',

  b. LagNNA as LagNominalNetAssets Label = 'LagNominalNetAssets: UnAdjusted Net Assets Per Share at the end of Previous Quarter'

 from cnmarket.of_q as a left join work.lastdayofquarter as b

  on a.fundcd = b.fundcd and a.quarter = b.quarter

  order by a.fundcd, a.quarter;

 quit;

 data cnmarket.of_q (alter = password write = password);

  set cnmarket.of_q;

  if TotalShares = . then TotalShares = 0;

  if LagTotalShares = . then LagTotalShares = 0;

  if SharesIn = . then SharesIn = 0;

  if SharesOut = . then SharesOut = 0;

  if NetAssets = . then NetAssets = 0;

  if LagNetAssets = . then LagNetAssets = 0;

  if NominalNetAssets = . then NominalNetAssets = 0;

  if LagNominalNetAssets = . then LagNominalNetAssets = 0;

  if TotalShares = 0 and LagTotalShares ne 0 and (SharesIn ne 0 or SharesOut ne 0)

  then TotalShares = LagTotalShares + SharesIn - SharesOut;

  if LagTotalShares = 0 and TotalShares ne 0 and (SharesIn ne 0 or SharesOut ne 0)

```
    then LagTotalShares = TotalShares - SharesIn + SharesOut;
    AvgTotalShares = (TotalShares + LagTotalShares) /2;
    if ( SharesIn = 0 or SharesOut = 0 ) and TotalShares ne 0 and LagTotalShares ne 0
    then SharesChange = TotalShares-LagTotalShares;
    else SharesChange = SharesIn-SharesOut;
    if AvgTotalShares ne 0 then do;
     PctSharesIn = SharesIn /AvgTotalShares;
     PctSharesOut = SharesOut /AvgTotalShares;
     PctSharesChange = SharesChange /AvgTotalShares;
    end;
    TNA = NominalNetAssets * TotalShares;
    LagTNA = LagNominalNetAssets * LagTotalShares;
    AvgTNA = (TNA + LagTNA) /2;
    CashInFlow = SharesIn * (NominalNetAssets + Lag-NominalNetAssets) /2;
    CashOutFlow = SharesOut * (NominalNetAssets + Lag-NominalNetAssets) /2;
    CashNetFlow2 = CashInFlow-CashOutFlow;
    CashNetFlow = TNA-(1 + Return) * LagTNA;
    if CashNetFlow = . or CashNetFlow = 0 then CashNetFlow = CashNetFlow2;
    if AvgTNA ne 0 then do;
     PctCashInFlow = CashInFlow /AvgTNA;
     PctCashOutFlow = CashOutFlow /AvgTNA;
     PctCashNetFlow = CashNetFlow /AvgTNA;
```

```
        end;
    if TotalShares >0 then LogTotalShares = log (Total-
Shares); else LogTotalShares = 0;
    if LagTotalShares > 0 then LogLagTotalShares = log
(LagTotalShares); else LogLagTotalShares = 0;
    if SharesOut > 0 then LogSharesOut = log (SharesOut);
else LogSharesOut = 0;
    if SharesIn > 0 then LogSharesIn = log (SharesIn);
else LogSharesIn = 0;
    if SharesChange >0 then LogSharesChange = log (Shares-
Change); else LogSharesChange = 0;
    if TNA >0 then LogTNA = log (TNA); else LogTNA = 0;
    if LagTNA > 0 then LogLagTNA = log (LagTNA); else
LogLagTNA = 0;
    if CashInFlow >0 then LogCashInFlow = log (CashInFlow);
else LogCashInFlow = 0;
    if CashOutFlow >0 then LogCashOutFlow = log (CashOutFlow);
else LogCashOutFlow = 0;
    if CashNetFlow >0 then LogCashNetFlow = log (CashNet-
Flow); else LogCashNetFlow = 0;
    format SharesChange AvgTotalShares SharesChange TNA
LagTNA CashInFlow CashOutFlow CashNetFlow2 CashNetFlow
AvgTNA comma32.;
    format  PctSharesIn  PctSharesOut  PctSharesChange
PctCashInFlow PctCashOutFlow PctCashNetFlow percent8.4;
    Label SharesChange = 'SharesChange: Total Number of
Shares Changed during the Quarter. SharesIn-SharesOut';
```

Label AvgTotalShares = 'AvgTotalShares: Average Number of Shares During the Quarter';

Label SharesChange = 'SharesChange: Total Number of Shares Changed during the Quarter. SharesIn-SharesOut';

Label PctSharesIn = 'PctSharesIn: Percentage Shares Inflow Relative to Average Number of Shares During the Quarter';

Label PctSharesOut = 'PctSharesOut: Percentage Shares Outflow Relative to Average Number of Shares During the Quarter';

Label PctSharesChange = 'PctSharesChange: Percentage Shares Changed during the Quarter Relative to Average Number of Shares During the Quarter';

Label TNA = 'TNA: Total Net Assets at the end of the Quarter';

Label LagTNA = 'LagTNA: Total Net Assets at the end of previous Quarter';

Label AvgTNA = 'AvgTNA: Average TNA during the quarter';

Label CashInFlow = 'CashInFlow: Cash flow into the fund';

Label CashOutFlow = 'CashOutFlow: Cash flow out of the fund';

Label CashNetFlow2 = 'CashNetFlow2: Net Cash flow into the fund, CashInflow-CashOutflow';

Label CashNetFlow = 'CashNetFlow: Net Cash flow into the fund';

Label PctCashInFlow = 'PctCashInFlow: Cash Inflow relative to AvgTNA';

```
   Label PctCashOutFlow = 'PctCashOutFlow: Cash Outflow relative to AvgTNA';
   Label PctCashNetFlow = 'PctCashNetFlow: Cash Netflow relative to AvgTNA';
  run;

  proc datasets library=work nolist;
   delete Lastdayofquarter test x x1 sharechg ;
  run;quit;
```

7

Market Microstructure Research

7.1 Research on Decomposing Bid-ask Spread and Estimating PIN

Market microstructure study is by every means the most challenging data-processing task in financial researches. That is because market microstructure tries to decipher the patterns hidden in tick-by-tick data of trades and quotes. The first invented and the most widely used measures aiming to unveil these hidden patterns from trades and quotes data are the decomposition of bid-ask spread and the measure of PIN. The following is a brief discussion of the research about these measures.

Glosten and Milgrom (1985) study the bid–ask spread from the perspective of quotation revision dynamics. The key assumption/conclusion is that the market maker updates the quote after every trade occurs. A buy order leads an upward updating of the ask price, and a sell order leads a downward updating for the bid price. In words, market maker is updating their quotation as if next order comes from an informed investor, although in a probabilistic view. Thus, the amount of updating depends on the market maker's expected probability of next order's being informed. Notice that this quotation updating feature can also be well explained by Ho and Stoll (1981) and O'Hara and Oldfield (1986). Glosten et al. (1985) formalize the quotation revision dynamics, which explains how the private information is assimilated by the market. The market maker updates the bid and ask prices after every transaction occurs as if the order is placed by an informed trader. (In this sense, the model of Glosten et al. (1985) has some Bayesian flavor.) The price will be updated to the point that equates the informed trader's expectation conditioning on his private information.

Easley and O'Hara (1987) contend that trade size plays roles when market makers set prices. The general idea is that, for multiple informed traders, trading large size always (weakly) dominates other actions. Thus trading size is naturally related to informed trading. Taking this into account, market makers update their belief and therefore set prices by observing the trade size. They work out two equilibrium, namely pooling equilibrium and separating equilibrium. In separating equilibrium, the informed traders always trade large size. To formalize the conditions for the existence of pooling and separating equilibrium, the authors propose two concepts: market width and depth. The former refers to the ratio of large to small trade size. The latter refers to the fraction of large trades made by uninformed traders. When the market has sufficiently large width or few informed traders, the separating equilibrium will prevail; the pooling equilibrium will prevail otherwise.

Later on, researchers try to answer this question: Is liquidity beta a risk factor to be priced? There are two lines on this topic. One line of research argues that illiquidity is a risk factor, because investors holding illiquid stocks may find it hard to find the counter party to trade the stocks. Let us call this view as "illiquidity risk". This line of research finds expected returns are negatively related to various liquidity measures, for example the bid-ask spread by Amihud and Mendelson (1986), price impact by Brennan and Subrahmanyam (1996), turnover by Datar, Y. Naik and Radcliffe (1998), trading volume by Brennan, Chordia and Subrahmanyam (1998). The other line of research deals with the individual stock's sensitivity to market wide liquidity. Let us call this view as "liquidity beta." For example: Pástor and Stambaugh (2003). Can these two views be reconciled? Acharya and Pedersen (2005) and Korajczyk and Sadka (2008) provide evidence that both liquidity effects are priced. Interested readers can also see the following papers for further discussions on the topic: Pástor et al. (2003), Acharya et al. (2005), Sadka (2006), Bekaert, Harvey and Lundblad (2007), Korajczyk et al. (2008)

Stoll (2000) provides a summary of ideas behind bid-ask spread. Two branches, one is because of order processing and inventory costs; the other is because of asymmetric information. In Stoll's term, the former is the real friction, while the latter is the informational friction. Following this line, bid-ask spread can be decomposed into three parts: order handling costs, inventory costs, and the adverse selection costs. Van Ness and Warr (2001) summarize the five commonly used methods of decomposing bid-ask spread, which are Glosten and Harris (1988), George, Kaul and Nimalendran (1991) (modified by Neal and Wheatley (1998)), Lin, Sanger and Booth (1995), Madhavan, Richardson and Roomans (1997), Huang and Stoll (1997). Glosten et al. (1988)

decomposes bid – ask spread into asymmetric information costs and inventory costs/order processing costs/monopoly power. Huang et al. (1997) is the only one among these four models to decompose bid – ask spread into three components. Other models slump up order processing cost and inventory holding costs. Inventory holding costs are hard to estimate because they cause price to change in a similar way of adverse selection costs do.

The original PIN is defined in Easley, Kiefer and O'Hara et al. (1996), by maximizing the following likelihood function:

$$L = \prod \left[\frac{(1-\alpha)e^{-\varepsilon}\varepsilon^B}{B} \frac{e^{-\varepsilon}\varepsilon^S}{S} + \frac{\alpha\delta e^{-\varepsilon}\varepsilon^B}{B} \frac{e^{-(\mu+\varepsilon)}(\mu+\varepsilon)^S}{S} + \frac{\alpha(1-\delta)e^{-(\mu+\varepsilon)}(\mu+\varepsilon)^B}{B} \frac{e^{-\varepsilon}\varepsilon^S}{S} \right]$$

$$\text{PIN} = \frac{\alpha\mu}{\alpha\mu + 2\varepsilon} \qquad (1)$$

In equations (1), α denotes the probability that an informational event happens today, δ denotes the probability that the event reveals a negative signal of the firm value, ε denotes the number of orders from liquidity investors, μ denotes the number of orders from informed investors. To avoid large numbers in estimation, we define $f(k,\lambda) = \frac{\lambda^k e^{-\lambda}}{k}$ as the PDF of Poisson distribution (λ and k denote the expected and realized occurrence, respectively), and rewrite the above equation as

$$L = \prod \left[(1-\alpha)f(B,\varepsilon)f(S,\varepsilon) + \alpha\delta f(B,\varepsilon)f[S,(\mu+\varepsilon)] + \alpha(1-\delta)f[B,(\mu+\varepsilon)]f(S,\varepsilon) \right] \qquad (2)$$

In Easley, Hvidkjaer and O'Hara (2002), the likelihood function is slightly different. In Duarte and Young (2009), they further revise the PIN model. The differences are as follows. 1) Allowing that the number of buy orders from informed investors are unequal to that of sell orders. The authors explain this revision by "account [ing] for the fact that in the data, buy order flows has a larger variance than sell order flow for almost all firms." Therefore, instead of using μ, the model uses μ_b and μ_s to denote the buy and sell order flow from informed investors, respectively. 2) Allowing that an event may increase both buy and sell order flows, perhaps because informed investors have heterogeneous interpretation of the signal. The authors call this event a "symmetric order-flow shock." Therefore, a new parameter θ is added to the model, representing the probability that event is such a symmetric order-flow shock. And when such an event happens, buy orders and sell orders increase by Δ_b and Δ_s.

The likelihood function to maximize is:

$$L = \prod \begin{bmatrix} (1-\alpha)(1-\theta)e^{-\varepsilon_b}\dfrac{\varepsilon_b^B}{B!}e^{-\varepsilon_s}\dfrac{\varepsilon_s^S}{S!} + \\ (1-\alpha)\theta e^{-(\varepsilon_b+\Delta_b)}\dfrac{(\varepsilon_b+\Delta_b)^B}{B!}e^{-(\varepsilon_s+\Delta_s)}\dfrac{(\varepsilon_s+\Delta_s)^S}{S!} + \\ \alpha(1-\theta)\delta e^{-\varepsilon_b}\dfrac{\varepsilon_b^B}{B!}e^{-(\mu_s+\varepsilon_s)}\dfrac{(\mu_s+\varepsilon_s)^S}{S!} + \\ \alpha\theta\delta e^{-(\varepsilon_b+\Delta_b)}\dfrac{(\varepsilon_b+\Delta_b)^B}{B!}e^{-(\mu_s+\varepsilon_s+\Delta_s)}\dfrac{(\mu_s+\varepsilon_s+\Delta_s)^S}{S!} + \\ \alpha(1-\theta)(1-\delta)e^{-(\mu_b+\varepsilon_b)}\dfrac{(\mu_b+\varepsilon_b)^B}{B!}e^{-\varepsilon_s}\dfrac{\varepsilon_s^S}{S!} + \\ \alpha\theta(1-\delta)e^{-(\mu_b+\varepsilon_b+\Delta_b)}\dfrac{(\mu_b+\varepsilon_b+\Delta_b)^B}{B!}e^{-(\varepsilon_s+\Delta_s)}\dfrac{(\varepsilon_s+\Delta_s)^S}{S!} \end{bmatrix}$$

$$= \prod \begin{bmatrix} (1-\alpha)(1-\theta)f(B,\varepsilon_b)f(S,\varepsilon_s) + \\ (1-\alpha)\theta f[B,(\varepsilon_b+\Delta_b)]f[S,(\varepsilon_s+\Delta_s)] + \\ \alpha(1-\theta)\delta f(B,\varepsilon_b)f[S,(\mu_s+\varepsilon_s)] + \\ \alpha\theta\delta f[B,(\varepsilon_b+\Delta_b)]f[S,(\mu_s+\varepsilon_s+\Delta_s)] + \\ \alpha(1-\theta)(1-\delta)f[B,(\mu_b+\varepsilon_b)]f(S,\varepsilon_s) + \\ \alpha\theta(1-\delta)f[B,(\mu_b+\varepsilon_b+\Delta_b)]f[S,(\varepsilon_s+\Delta_s)] \end{bmatrix}$$

(3)

The PIN is defined as

$$\text{AdjPIN} = \frac{\alpha[(1-\delta)\mu_b + \delta\mu_s]}{\alpha[(1-\delta)\mu_b + \delta\mu_s] + (\Delta_b + \Delta_s)[\alpha\theta + (1-\alpha)\theta] + \varepsilon_s + \varepsilon_b} \tag{4}$$

They also introduce a new probability PSOS, which is defined as

$$\text{PSOS} = \frac{(\Delta_b + \Delta_s)[\alpha\theta + (1-\alpha)\theta]}{\alpha[(1-\delta)\mu_b + \delta\mu_s] + (\Delta_b + \Delta_s)[\alpha\theta + (1-\alpha)\theta] + \varepsilon_s + \varepsilon_b} \tag{5}$$

PSOS is "the unconditional probability that a given trade will come from a shock to both buy and the sell order flows." The authors argue that PSOS is "effectively a proxy for illiquidity."

As for the implication of PIN, Easley and O'Hara (2004) argue that PIN can explain expected return, because it's a proxy of asymmetric information. The following paper also discusses the relation between asymmetric information and asset pricing: Easley et al. (2002), O'Hara (2003). Duarte et al. (2009) counter-argue that PIN is priced not because it's a proxy of asymmetric information, but because it's a proxy of illiquidity. These models do not account for the order size. Bernhardt and Hughson (2002) do.

7.2 Estimating the Microstructure Measures

Before discussing the coding issues of microstructure data, the readers need to familiarize themselves with the formats of the data. For the Chinese microstructure data, the major database providers are CSMAR, RESSET, and Thomson Tick History. For the U.S. microstructure data, the major database provider is TAQ of WRDS. Different database providers surely have different formats. But generally speaking, the most original microstructure data are comprised of two tables, namely the trade table and the quote table. The trade table records every execution of the trades. The quote table records every change in the bid and ask quotes. To process the microstructure data, the first job is to combine these two tables. After combining the two tables, we proceed to identify the executions as either buyer initiated or seller initiated, hence buy order and sell orders for short (see Lee and Ready (1991) for the identifications). The decomposition of bid-ask spreads and the estimation of PIN can only begin after the aforementioned jobs are done. The following codes cover the decomposition of spreads and the estimation of PIN, assuming the trades and quotes having been merged and processed properly.

```
% macro baspin (year = );


% put --decompose the bid-ask spread and Compute PIN--;
/* ---------Decompose the bid-ask spread ---------
--------------------------*/
ods listing close;
% let LogFile = % unquote ( % str(%')/research/bit_HY/
Log/Log&Year..Log% str(%') );
options nonotes nosource nosource2 errors = 0;
proc printto; run;
data _null_; % let rc = % sysfunc(filename(sas_log,
&LogFile)); % if &rc = 0 and % sysfunc(fexist(&sas_log)) %
then % let rc = % sysfunc(fdelete(&sas_log)); % let rc = %
sysfunc(filename(sas_log)); run;
options notes source source2 errors = 20;
proc printto log = &LogFile; run;
```

```sas
%macro bas(frequency=);
    %let data_in = cnintra.Y&year;
    %let data_in_mean = win.sum&year._&frequency;
    %let MeanPrice = Md_Price;
    %let MedianSize = Md_SharesTraded;
    %let MeanEBAS = Md_EffectiveSpread;
    %let MeanEBAS_Type = Full;
    %let data_out = cnintra.Bas&year._&frequency;
    %let Out_Spd_Type = Full;
    %let by_var1 = SecurityID;
    %if &frequency = m %then %do; %let by_var2 = month; %end;
    %else %if &frequency = q %then %do; %let by_var2 = quarter; %end;
    %else %if &frequency = s %then %do; %let by_var2 = semiyear; %end;
    %else %if &frequency = a %then %do; %let by_var2 = year; %end;
    %let by_var3 = %str();
    %let n_by_vars = 2;
    %let MP_dif = MP_Dif;
    %let TP_dif = TP_Dif;
    %let LogTP_dif = TP_LogDif;
    %let Sign = Sign;
    %let LagSign = LagSign;
    %let Lag2Sign = Lag2Sign;
    %let QuotedSpread = QuotedSpread;
```

```
%let LagQS = LagQS;
%let Lag2QS = Lag2QS;
%let PctSpd_Type = Full;
%let PctSpread = PctSpread;
%let EffSpd_Type = Full;
%let SignedEffSpd = SignedES;
%let LagSignedEffSpd = LagSignedES;
%let NormalizedV = yes;
%let Volume = NmShTd;
%let LagVolume = LagNmShTd;
%let Lag2Volume = Lag2NmShTd;

%let by_vars = &by_var1 &by_var2 &by_var3;
%if &n_by_vars = 1 %then %do;
  %let cond = %str(a.&by_var1 = b.&by_var1);
  %let keepvars = &by_var1;
%end;
%else %if &n_by_vars = 2 %then %do;
  %let cond = %str(a.&by_var1 = b.&by_var1 and a.&by_var2 = b.&by_var2);
  %let keepvars = %str(&by_var1 &by_var2);
%end;
%else %if &n_by_vars = 3 %then %do;
  %let cond = %str(a.&by_var1 = b.&by_var1 and a.&by_var2 = b.&by_var2 and a.&by_var3 = b.&by_var3);
  %let keepvars = %str(&by_var1 &by_var2 &by_var3);
%end;
```

```
/* ------------------HY 1 -------------------- */
    ods output ParameterEstimates = work._HY1_est;
    proc model data = &data_in;
      parms r0 r1 c0 c1 z0 z1;
        exogenous  &LagSign  &Lag2Sign  &LagVolume  &Lag2Volume;
        endogenous &Sign &MP_dif &TP_dif ;
        &Sign = ( r0 + r1 * &LagVolume ) * &LagSign;
        &MP_dif = ( z0 + z1 * &LagVolume ) * ( &LagSign-( r0 + r1 * &Lag2Volume ) * &Lag2Sign );
        &TP_dif = ( c0 + c1 * &LagVolume ) * &Sign + ( z0 + z1 * &LagVolume - c0 - c1 * &Lag2Volume ) * &LagSign - ( z0 + z1 * &LagVolume ) * ( r0 + r1 * &Lag2Volume ) * &Lag2Sign;
      fit &Sign &MP_dif &TP_dif /gmm outest = work._HY10_;
      by &by_vars;
    run; quit;
/* ------------------Huang and Stoll ---------------------- */
    ods output ParameterEstimates = work._hs_est;
    proc model data = &data_in;
      parms alpha beta pi;
      endogenous &LagSign &MP_dif;
      exogenous &LagQS &Lag2Sign &Lag2QS ;
      &LagSign = ( 1-2 * pi ) * &Lag2Sign;
      &MP_dif = ( ( alpha + beta ) * &LagQS * &LagSign )/ 2 - ( alpha * ( 1-2 * pi ) * &Lag2QS * &Lag2Sign ) /2;
```

```
      fit &LagSign &MP_dif /gmm outest = work._hs0_;
      by &by_vars;
   run; quit;
   /* ----------------- MRR ----------------- - -
- - - */
   ods output ParameterEstimates = work._mrr_est;
   proc model data = &data_in;
      parms phi theta rho;
      endogenous &sign &TP_dif;
      exogenous &LagSign &Lag2Sign;
      &TP_dif = theta * &sign + phi * (&sign - &LagSign) - rho
* theta * &Lag2Sign;
      &sign = rho * &LagSign;
      fit &sign &TP_dif /gmm outest = work._mrr0_;
      by &by_vars;
   run; quit;
   /* ----------------- LSB ----------------- */
   ods output ParameterEstimates = work._lsb_est;
   proc model data = &data_in;
      parms lambda  theta gamma;
      exogenous &LagSignedEffSpd;
      endogenous &MP_dif &SignedEffSpd &TP_dif;
      restrict gamma + lambda + theta = 1 ;
      % if % UPCASE (&EffSpd_Type) = % UPCASE (Full) % then
% do;
         &MP_dif = lambda * &LagSignedEffSpd /2;
         &SignedEffSpd = theta * &LagSignedEffSpd /2;
```

```sas
         &TP_dif =-gamma * &LagSignedEffSpd /2;
      % end;
      % else % do;
         &MP_dif = lambda * &LagSignedEffSpd ;
         &SignedEffSpd = theta * &LagSignedEffSpd ;
         &TP_dif =-gamma * &LagSignedEffSpd ;
      % end;
      fit &MP_dif &SignedEffSpd &TP_dif /gmm outest = work._lsb0_;
      by &by_vars;
   run; quit;
   /* ------------------GKN-------------------*/
   ods output ParameterEstimates = work._GKN_est;
   proc model data = &data_in;
      parms pi0 pi ; exogenous &PctSpread &Sign &LagSign;
      endogenous &LogTP_dif ;
      % if % UPCASE (&PctSpd_Type) = % UPCASE (Full) % then % do;
         &LogTP_dif =pi0 +pi * &PctSpread * (&Sign-&LagSign) /2 +(1-pi) * &PctSpread * &Sign /2;
      % end;
      % else % do;
         &LogTP _ dif = pi0 + pi * &PctSpread * (&Sign - &LagSign) +(1-pi) * &PctSpread * &Sign;
      % end;
      fit &LogTP_dif /gmm outest = work._GKN0_;
      by &by_vars;
```

```
    run; quit;
    /* ----------------Glosten-Harris----------
-----------*/
    ods output ParameterEstimates=work._gh_est;
    proc model data=&data_in;
       parms c0 c1 z0 z1;
       exogenous &Sign &LagSign &Volume &LagVolume;
       endogenous &TP_dif ;
         &TP_dif = c0 * (&Sign-&LagSign) + c1 * (&Sign *
&Volume-&LagSign * &LagVolume) + z0 * &Sign + z1 * &Sign
* &Volume;
       fit &TP_dif /gmm outest=work._gh0_;
       by &by_vars;
    run; quit;


    /* -------------------------COMPILE RESULTS---
--------------------------------*/
    /* ----------------HY 1-------------------
--*/
    data work._HY10_ (drop=_STATUS_ rename=(R0 = HY1_R0
R1 = HY1_R1 C0 = HY1_C0 C1 = HY1_C1 Z0 = HY1_Z0 Z1 = HY1_Z1));
       set work._HY10_ (where=(_STATUS_ like '% Converged%')
drop=_NAME_ _TYPE_ rename=( _NUSED_ = HY1_OBS ) );
       Label HY1_OBS='HY1_OBS: Observations Used in HY1';
       format HY1_OBS comma.;
    run;
    data work._HY1_R0 work._HY1_R1 work._HY1_C0 work._HY1_
```

```
C1 work._HY1_Z0 work._HY1_Z1;
    set work._HY1_est ;
    if Parameter = 'r0' then output work._HY1_R0;
    if Parameter = 'r1' then output work._HY1_R1;
    if Parameter = 'c0' then output work._HY1_C0;
    if Parameter = 'c1' then output work._HY1_C1;
    if Parameter = 'z0' then output work._HY1_Z0;
    if Parameter = 'z1' then output work._HY1_Z1;
  run;
  proc sql;
    create table work._HY1_ as
    select a.*,
      b.StdErr as HY1_C0_StdErr Label = 'HY1_C0_StdErr: HY1 C0 (Order Processing) Std Err',
      b.tValue as HY1_C0_tValue Label = 'HY1_C0_tValue: HY1 C0 (Order Processing) t-Value',
      b.Probt as HY1_C0_Probt Label = 'HY1_C0_Probt: HY1 C0 (Order Processing) p-Value'
    from work._HY10_ as a left join work._HY1_C0 as b
    on &cond;

    create table work._HY1_ as
    select a.*,
      b.StdErr as HY1_C1_StdErr Label = 'HY1_C1_StdErr: HY1 C1 (Order Processing) Std Err',
      b.tValue as HY1_C1_tValue Label = 'HY1_C1_tValue: HY1 C1 (Order Processing) t-Value',
```

```
        b.Probt as HY1_C1_Probt Label = 'HY1_C1_Probt: HY1 C1
(Order Processing) p-Value'
        from work._HY1_ as a left join work._HY1_C1 as b
        on &cond;


        create table work._HY1_ as
        select a.*,
          b.StdErr as HY1_Z0_StdErr Label = 'HY1_Z0_StdErr: HY1
Z0 (Adverse Selection) Std Err',
          b.tValue as HY1_Z0_tValue Label = 'HY1_Z0_tValue: HY1
Z0 (Adverse Selection) t-Value',
          b.Probt as HY1_Z0_Probt Label = 'HY1_Z0_Probt: HY1 Z0
(Adverse Selection) p-Value'
        from work._HY1_ as a left join work._HY1_Z0 as b
        on &cond;


        create table work._HY1_ as
        select a.*,
          b.StdErr as HY1_Z1_StdErr Label = 'HY1_Z1_StdErr: HY1
Z1 (Adverse Selection) Std Err',
          b.tValue as HY1_Z1_tValue Label = 'HY1_Z1_tValue: HY1
Z1 (Adverse Selection) t-Value',
          b.Probt as HY1_Z1_Probt Label = 'HY1_Z1_Probt: HY1 Z1
(Adverse Selection) p-Value'
        from work._HY1_ as a left join work._HY1_Z1 as b
        on &cond;
```

```
        create table work._HY1_ as
        select a.*,
            b.StdErr as HY1_R0_StdErr Label = 'HY1_R0_StdErr: HY1
R0 (Serial Order Correlation) Std Err',
            b.tValue as HY1_R0_tValue Label = 'HY1_R0_tValue: HY1
R0 (Serial Order Correlation) t-Value',
            b.Probt as HY1_R0_Probt Label = 'HY1_R0_Probt: HY1 R0
(Serial Order Correlation) p-Value'
        from work._HY1_ as a left join work._HY1_R0 as b
        on &cond;

        create table work._HY1_ as
        select a.*,
            b.StdErr as HY1_R1_StdErr Label = 'HY1_R1_StdErr: HY1
R1 (Serial Order Correlation) Std Err',
            b.tValue as HY1_R1_tValue Label = 'HY1_R1_tValue: HY1
R1 (Serial Order Correlation) t-Value',
            b.Probt as HY1_R1_Probt Label = 'HY1_R1_Probt: HY1 R1
(Serial Order Correlation) p-Value'
        from work._HY1_ as a left join work._HY1_R1 as b
        on &cond;
    quit;
    /* ------------------ Huang and Stoll -----------
----------- */
    data work._hs0_ ( drop = _STATUS_ rename = ( Alpha = HS_
Alpha Beta = HS_Beta pi = HS_pi ) );
        set work._hs0_ ( where = (_STATUS_ like '% Converged%')
```

```
drop = _NAME_ _TYPE_ rename = ( _NUSED_ = HS_OBS ) );
    Label HS_OBS = 'HS_OBS: Observations Used in Huang-
Stoll';
    format HS_OBS comma.;
  run;

  data work._hs_alpha work._hs_beta work._hs_pi;
    set work._hs_est ;
    if Parameter = 'alpha' then output work._hs_alpha;
    if Parameter = 'beta' then output work._hs_beta;
    if Parameter = 'pi' then output work._hs_pi;
  run;

  proc sql;
    create table work._hs_ as
    select a.*,
      b.StdErr as HS_Alpha_StdErr Label = 'HS_Alpha_StdErr:
Huang-Stoll Alpha (Adverse Selection) Std Err',
      b.tValue as HS_Alpha_tValue Label = 'HS_Alpha_tValue:
Huang-Stoll Alpha (Adverse Selection) t-Value',
      b.Probt as HS_Alpha_Probt Label = 'HS_Alpha_Probt:
Huang-Stoll Alpha (Adverse Selection) p-Value'
    from work._hs0_ as a left join work._hs_alpha as b
    on &cond;

    create table work._hs_ as
    select a.*,
```

```
        b.StdErr as HS_Beta_StdErr Label ='HS_Beta_StdErr:
Huang-Stoll Beta (Inventory Holding) Std Err',
        b.tValue as HS_Beta_tValue Label ='HS_Beta_tValue:
Huang-Stoll Beta (Inventory Holding) t-Value',
        b.Probt as HS_Beta_Probt Label ='HS_Beta_Probt: Huang-
Stoll Beta (Inventory Holding) p-Value'
      from work._hs_ as a left join work._hs_Beta as b
      on &cond;

      create table work._hs_ as
      select a.*,
        b.StdErr as HS_Pi_StdErr Label ='HS_Pi_StdErr: Huang-
Stoll Pi (Order Reversal) Std Err',
        b.tValue as HS_Pi_tValue Label ='HS_Pi_tValue: Huang-
Stoll Pi (Order Reversal) t-Value',
        b.Probt as HS_Pi_Probt Label ='HS_Pi_Probt: Huang-
Stoll Pi (Order Reversal) p-Value'
      from work._hs_ as a left join work._hs_pi as b
      on &cond;
   quit;
   /* ------------------MRR--------------------*/
   data work._mrr0_ ( drop =_STATUS_ rename =( phi = MRR_
phi Theta =MRR_Theta rho =MRR_Rho));
      set work._MRR0_ ( where =(_STATUS_ like '% Converged%')
drop =_NAME__TYPE_ rename =(_NUSED_=MRR_OBS ) );
      Label MRR_OBS ='MRR_OBS: Observations Used in MRR';
      format MRR_OBS comma.;
```

```
run;

data work._MRR_phi work._MRR_Theta work._MRR_Rho;
  set work._MRR_est ;
  if Parameter ='phi' then output work._MRR_phi;
  if Parameter ='theta' then output work._MRR_Theta;
  if Parameter ='rho' then output work._MRR_rho;
run;

proc sql;
  create table work._MRR_ as
  select a.*,
    b.StdErr as MRR_Phi_StdErr Label = 'MRR_Phi_StdErr: MRR Phi (Order Processing) Std Err',
    b.tValue as MRR_Phi_tValue Label = 'MRR_Phi_tValue: MRR Phi (Order Processing) t-Value',
    b.Probt as MRR_Phi_Probt Label = 'MRR_Phi_Probt: MRR Phi (Order Processing) p-Value'
  from work._MRR0_ as a left join work._MRR_Phi as b
  on &cond;

  create table work._MRR_ as
  select a.*,
    b.StdErr as MRR_Theta_StdErr Label = 'MRR_Theta_StdErr: MRR Theta (Adverse Selection) Std Err',
    b.tValue as MRR_Theta_tValue Label = 'MRR_Theta_tValue: MRR Theta (Adverse Selection) t-Value',
```

```
        b.Probt as MRR_Theta_Probt Label = 'MRR_Theta_Probt:
MRR Theta (Adverse Selection) p-Value'
            from work._MRR_ as a left join work._MRR_Theta as b
            on &cond;

            create table work._MRR_ as
            select a.*,
            b.StdErr as MRR_Rho_StdErr Label = 'MRR_Rho_StdErr:
MRR Rho (Serial Order Correlation) Std Err',
                b.tValue as MRR_Rho_tValue Label = 'MRR_Rho_tValue:
MRR Rho (Serial Order Correlation) t-Value',
                b.Probt as MRR_Rho_Probt Label = 'MRR_Rho_Probt: MRR
Rho (Serial Order Correlation) p-Value'
            from work._MRR_ as a left join work._MRR_Rho as b
            on &cond;
        quit;
        /*------------------LSB---------------------*/
        data work._LSB0_ ( drop =_STATUS_ rename = ( Gamma = LSB_
Gamma Theta = LSB_Theta Lambda = LSB_Lambda ) );
            set work._LSB0_ ( where = (_STATUS_ like '% Converged%')
drop =_NAME_ _TYPE_ rename = ( _NUSED_ = LSB_OBS ) );
            Label LSB_OBS ='LSB_OBS: Observations Used in LSB';
            format LSB_OBS comma.;
        run;


        data work._LSB_Gamma work._LSB_Theta work._LSB_
Lambda;
```

```
   set work._LSB_est ;
   if Parameter = 'gamma' then output work._LSB_Gamma;
   if Parameter = 'theta' then output work._LSB_Theta;
   if Parameter = 'lambda' then output work._LSB_Lambda;
run;

proc sql;
   create table work._LSB_ as
   select a.*,
      b.StdErr as LSB_Gamma_StdErr Label = 'LSB_Gamma_StdErr: LSB Gamma (Order Processing) Std Err',
      b.tValue as LSB_Gamma_tValue Label = 'LSB_Gamma_tValue: LSB Gamma (Order Processing) t-Value',
      b.Probt as LSB_Gamma_Probt Label = 'LSB_Gamma_Probt: LSB Gamma (Order Processing) p-Value'
      from work._LSB0_ as a left join work._LSB_Gamma as b
      on &cond;

   create table work._LSB_ as
   select a.*,
      b.StdErr as LSB_Theta_StdErr Label = 'LSB_Theta_StdErr: LSB Theta (Serial Order Correlation) Std Err',
      b.tValue as LSB_Theta_tValue Label = 'LSB_Theta_tValue: LSB Theta (Serial Order Correlation) t-Value',
      b.Probt as LSB_Theta_Probt Label = 'LSB_Theta_Probt: LSB Theta (Serial Order Correlation) p-Value'
      from work._LSB_ as a left join work._LSB_Theta as b
```

```
    on &cond;


    create table work._LSB_ as
    select a.*,
        b.StdErr as LSB_Lambda_StdErr Label = 'LSB_Lambda_
StdErr: LSB Lambda (Adverse Selection) Std Err',
        b.tValue as LSB_Lambda_tValue Label = 'LSB_Lambda_
tValue: LSB Lambda (Adverse Selection) t-Value',
        b.Probt as LSB_Lambda_Probt Label = 'LSB_Lambda_
Probt: LSB Lambda (Adverse Selection) p-Value'
    from work._LSB_ as a left join work._LSB_Lambda as b
    on &cond;
quit;
/* ------------------GKN---------------------- */
data work._GKN0_ (drop=_STATUS_ rename=(pi0=GKN_Pi0
pi=GKN_Pi));
    set work._GKN0_ (where=(_STATUS_ like '%Converged%')
drop=_NAME_ _TYPE_ rename=( _NUSED_=GKN_OBS ));
    Label GKN_OBS='GKN_OBS: Observations Used in GKN';
    format GKN_OBS comma.;
run;
data work._GKN_Pi0 work._GKN_Pi ;
    set work._GKN_est ;
    if Parameter='pi0' then output work._GKN_Pi0;
    if Parameter='pi' then output work._GKN_Pi;
run;
```

```
   proc sql;
     create table work._GKN_ as
     select a.*,
       b.StdErr as GKN_Pi0_StdErr Label = 'GKN_Pi0_StdErr:
GKN Pi0 (Expected Return) Std Err',
       b.tValue as GKN_Pi0_tValue Label = 'GKN_Pi0_tValue:
GKN Pi0 (Expected Return) t-Value',
       b.Probt as GKN_Pi0_Probt Label = 'GKN_Pi0_Probt: GKN
Pi0 (Expected Return) p-Value'
     from work._GKN0_ as a left join work._GKN_Pi0 as b
     on &cond;

     create table work._GKN_ as
     select a.*,
       b.StdErr as GKN_Pi_StdErr Label = 'GKN_Pi_StdErr: GKN
Pi (Order Processing) Std Err',
       b.tValue as GKN_Pi_tValue Label = 'GKN_Pi_tValue: GKN
Pi (Order Processing) t-Value',
       b.Probt as GKN_Pi_Probt Label = 'GKN_Pi_Probt: GKN Pi
(Order Processing) p-Value'
     from work._GKN_ as a left join work._GKN_Pi as b
     on &cond;
   quit;
   /* ------------------Glosten-Harris----------
------------ */
   data work._GH0_ ( drop = _STATUS_ rename = ( C0 = GH_C0 C1
= GH_C1 Z0 = GH_Z0 Z1 = GH_Z1 ) );
```

```
    set work._GH0_ (where = (_STATUS_ like '% Converged% ')
drop = _NAME_ _TYPE_ rename = (_NUSED_ = GH_OBS));
        Label GH_OBS = 'GH_OBS: Observations Used in GH';
        format GH_OBS comma.;
    run;
    data work._GH_C0 work._GH_C1 work._GH_Z0 work._GH_Z1;
        set work._GH_est ;
        if Parameter = 'c0' then output work._GH_C0;
        if Parameter = 'c1' then output work._GH_C1;
        if Parameter = 'z0' then output work._GH_Z0;
        if Parameter = 'z1' then output work._GH_Z1;
    run;
    proc sql;
        create table work._GH_ as
        select a.*,
        b.StdErr as GH_C0_StdErr Label = 'GH_C0_StdErr: GH C0
(Order Processing) Std Err',
        b.tValue as GH_C0_tValue Label = 'GH_C0_tValue: GH C0
(Order Processing) t-Value',
        b.Probt as GH_C0_Probt Label = 'GH_C0_Probt: GH C0
(Order Processing) p-Value'
        from work._GH0_ as a left join work._GH_C0 as b
        on &cond;

        create table work._GH_ as
        select a.*,
        b.StdErr as GH_C1_StdErr Label = 'GH_C1_StdErr: GH C1
```

```
(Order Processing) Std Err',
      b.tValue as GH_C1_tValue Label = 'GH_C1_tValue: GH C1
(Order Processing) t-Value',
      b.Probt as GH_C1_Probt Label = 'GH_C1_Probt: GH C1
(Order Processing) p-Value'
      from work._GH_ as a left join work._GH_C1 as b
      on &cond;


   create table work._GH_ as
   select a.*,
      b.StdErr as GH_Z0_StdErr Label = 'GH_Z0_StdErr: GH Z0
(Adverse Selection) Std Err',
      b.tValue as GH_Z0_tValue Label = 'GH_Z0_tValue: GH Z0
(Adverse Selection) t-Value',
      b.Probt as GH_Z0_Probt Label = 'GH_Z0_Probt: GH Z0
(Adverse Selection) p-Value'
      from work._GH_ as a left join work._GH_Z0 as b
      on &cond;


   create table work._GH_ as
   select a.*,
      b.StdErr as GH_Z1_StdErr Label = 'GH_Z1_StdErr: GH Z1
(Adverse Selection) Std Err',
      b.tValue as GH_Z1_tValue Label = 'GH_Z1_tValue: GH Z1
(Adverse Selection) t-Value',
      b.Probt as GH_Z1_Probt Label = 'GH_Z1_Probt: GH Z1
(Adverse Selection) p-Value'
```

```
    from work._GH_ as a left join work._GH_Z1 as b
    on &cond;
quit;
*Combine All;
data work._alllist_;
    set work._HY1_(keep=&keepvars) work._hs_(keep=&keepvars) work._mrr_(keep=&keepvars)
        work._lsb_(keep=&keepvars) work._gkn_(keep=&keepvars) work._gh_(keep=&keepvars);
run;
proc sort data = work._alllist_ out = &data_out nodupkey;
    by &by_vars;
run;

proc sql;
    create table &data_out as
    select a.*,
    b.HY1_OBS, b.HY1_R0 Label = 'HY1_R0: Parameter of Serial Order Correlation', b.HY1_R0_Probt, b.HY1_R0_StdErr, b.HY1_R0_tValue,
        b.HY1_R1 Label = 'HY1_R1: Parameter of Serial Order Correlation', b.HY1_R1_Probt, b.HY1_R1_StdErr, b.HY1_R1_tValue,
        b.HY1_C0 Label = 'HY1_C0: Parameter of Order Processing', b.HY1_C0_Probt, b.HY1_C0_StdErr, b.HY1_C0_tValue,
```

b.HY1_C1 Label = 'HY1_C1: Parameter of Order Processing', b.HY1_C1_Probt, b.HY1_C1_StdErr, b.HY1_C1_tValue,

b.HY1_Z0 Label = 'HY1_Z0: Parameter of Adverse Selection', b.HY1_Z0_Probt, b.HY1_Z0_StdErr, b.HY1_Z0_tValue,

b.HY1_Z1 Label = 'HY1_Z1: Parameter of Adverse Selection', b.HY1_Z1_Probt, b.HY1_Z1_StdErr, b.HY1_Z1_tValue

from &data_out as a left join work._HY1_ as b
on &cond;

create table &data_out as
select a.*,
b.HS_OBS, b.HS_Alpha Label = 'HS_Alpha: Parameter of Adverse Selection', b.HS_Alpha_Probt, b.HS_Alpha_StdErr, b.HS_Alpha_tValue,

b.HS_Beta Label = 'HS_Beta: Parameter of Inventory Holding', b.HS_Beta_Probt, b.HS_Beta_StdErr, b.HS_Beta_tValue,

b.HS_pi Label = 'HS_pi: Parameter of Order Reversal', b.HS_Pi_Probt, b.HS_Pi_StdErr, b.HS_Pi_tValue

from &data_out as a left join work._hs_ as b
on &cond;

create table &data_out as
select a.*,

```
        b.MRR_OBS, b.MRR_phi Label = 'MRR_phi: Parameter of
Order Processing', b.MRR_Phi_Probt, b.MRR_Phi_StdErr,
b.MRR_Phi_tValue,
        b.MRR_Rho Label = 'MRR_Rho: Parameter of Serial Order
Correlation', b.MRR_Rho_Probt, b.MRR_Rho_StdErr, b.MRR_
Rho_tValue,
        b.MRR_Theta Label = 'MRR_Theta: Parameter of Adverse
Selection', b.MRR_Theta_Probt, b.MRR_Theta_StdErr, b.MRR_
Theta_tValue
    from &data_out as a left join work._mrr_ as b
    on &cond;

    create table &data_out as
    select a.*,
        b.LSB_OBS, b.LSB_Gamma Label = 'LSB_Gamma: Parameter
of Order Processing', b.LSB_Gamma_Probt, b.LSB_Gamma_
StdErr, b.LSB_Gamma_tValue,
        b.LSB_Lambda Label = 'LSB_Lambda: Parameter of
Adverse Selection', b.LSB_Lambda_Probt, b.LSB_Lambda_
StdErr, b.LSB_Lambda_tValue,
        b.LSB_Theta Label = 'LSB_Theta: Parameter of Serial
Order Correlation', b.LSB_Theta_Probt, b.LSB_Theta_
StdErr, b.LSB_Theta_tValue
    from &data_out as a left join work._lsb_ as b
    on &cond;

    create table &data_out as
```

```
    select a.*,
  b.GKN_OBS, b.GKN_Pi0 Label = 'GKN_Pi0: Parameter of
Expected Return', b.GKN_Pi0_Probt, b.GKN_Pi0_StdErr, b.GKN_
Pi0_tValue,
     b.GKN_Pi Label = 'GKN_Pi: Parameter of Order
Processing', b.GKN_Pi_Probt, b.GKN_Pi_StdErr, b.GKN_Pi_
tValue
    from &data_out as a left join work._gkn_ as b
    on &cond;

  create table &data_out as
    select a.*,
  b.GH_OBS, b.GH_C0 Label = 'GH_C0: Parameter of Order
Processing', b.GH_C0_Probt, b.GH_C0_StdErr, b.GH_C0_
tValue,
    b.GH_C1 Label = 'GH_C1: Parameter of Order Processing',
b.GH_C1_Probt, b.GH_C1_StdErr, b.GH_C1_tValue,
     b.GH_Z0 Label = 'GH_Z0: Parameter of Adverse
Selection', b.GH_Z0_Probt, b.GH_Z0_StdErr, b.GH_Z0_tValue,
     b.GH_Z1 Label = 'GH_Z1: Parameter of Adverse
Selection', b.GH_Z1_Probt, b.GH_Z1_StdErr, b.GH_Z1_tValue
    from &data_out as a left join work._gh_ as b
    on &cond;

  create table &data_out as
      select  a.*, b. &MeanPrice, b. &MedianSize,
b.&MeanEBAS
```

```
       from &data_out as a left join &data_in_mean as b
       on &cond;
   quit;

   %mend bas;

   %bas(frequency=m) %put Month Finishes;
   %bas(frequency=q) %put Quarter Finishes;
   %bas(frequency=s) %put SemiYear Finishes;
   %bas(frequency=a) %put Year Finishes;

   %macro PIN(data_in=win.sum&year._d,
       buy_var=Cum_Buy_O,
       sell_var=Cum_Sell_O,
       by_var1=securityid,
       by_var2=,
       by_var3=,
       n_by_vars=2,
       data_out=,
       detail_out=no,
       n_estimation=10,
       random_range=300
   );

       %let by_vars=&by_var1 &by_var2 &by_var3;
       %if &n_by_vars=1 %then %do;
           %let cond=%str(a.&by_var1=b.&by_var1);
```

```
    % let byvars = a.&by_var1;
    % let byvars2 = &by_var1;
    % let firstbyvar = &by_var1;
  % end;
  % else % if &n_by_vars = 2 % then % do;
    % let cond = % str (a.&by_var1 = b.&by_var1 and a.&by_var2 = b.&by_var2);
    % let byvars = % str (a.&by_var1, a.&by_var2);
    % let byvars2 = % str (&by_var1, &by_var2);
    % let firstbyvar = &by_var2;
  % end;
  % else % if &n_by_vars = 3 % then % do;
    % let cond = % str (a.&by_var1 = b.&by_var1 and a.&by_var2 = b.&by_var2 and a.&by_var3 = b.&by_var3);
    % let byvars = % str (a.&by_var1, a.&by_var2, a.&by_var3);
    % let byvars2 = % str (&by_var1, &by_var2, &by_var3);
    % let firstbyvar = &by_var3;
  % end;

  data work._in_;
    set &data_in (keep = &by_vars &buy_var &sell_var);
    if &buy_var ne . and &sell_var ne .;
  run;
  data work._ini_;
    do Ini = 1 to &n_estimation;
    a = ranuni(0);
```

```
    q = ranuni(0);
    delta = ranuni(0);
    mu = ranuni(0) * &random_range;
    mu_b = ranuni(0) * &random_range;
    mu_s = ranuni(0) * &random_range;
    ep_b = ranuni(0) * &random_range;
    ep_s = ranuni(0) * &random_range;
    D_b = ranuni(0) * &random_range;
    D_s = ranuni(0) * &random_range;
    output;
  end;
run;
proc datasets library = work nolist;
  delete _fs1__est1_;
run;quit;

sasfile work._in_ open;
% do i =1 % to &n_estimation;
% put ------Estimate Time &i -----------;
data _null_;
  set work._ini_;
  if Ini = &i;
  call symput ( 'a', a );
  call symput ( 'q', q );
  call symput ( 'delta', delta );
  call symput ( 'mu', mu );
  call symput ( 'mu_b', mu_b);
```

```
    call symput ( 'mu_s', mu_s );
    call symput ( 'ep_b', ep_b );
    call symput ( 'ep_s', ep_s );
    call symput ( 'D_b', D_b );
    call symput ( 'D_s', D_s );
  run;

  ods output AdditionalEstimates =work._est_ FitStatistics =work._fs_ ;
  proc nlmixed data =work._in_ fd = central technique = quanew update =bfgs;
    by &by_vars;
    parms a =&a, delta =&delta, mu =&mu, ep_b =&ep_b, ep_s = &ep_s, ;
    bounds 0 <= a <=1, 0 <= delta <= 1, mu >=0, ep_b >= 0, ep_s >= 0;
    pin =a * mu /( a * mu + ep_b + ep_s );
    Lik = ( 1 - a ) * pdf ( 'poisson', &buy _ var, ep _ b ) * pdf ('poisson',&sell_var,ep_s)
        + a * delta * pdf ( 'poisson', &buy _ var, ep _ b ) * pdf ('poisson',&sell_var,mu +ep_s)
        + a * (1 -delta) * pdf('poisson',&buy_var,mu + ep_b) * pdf('poisson',&sell_var,ep_s);
    if Lik =0 then Lik =1E-300;
    LogLik = log( Lik );
    model &buy_var ~general ( LogLik );
    estimate 'alpha' a;
```

```
    estimate 'delta' delta ;
    estimate 'mu' mu;
    estimate 'buy_epsilon' ep_b;
    estimate 'sell_epsilon' ep_s;
    estimate 'PIN' pin;
run;
data work._est_;
 set work._est_;
 Ini = &i;
run;
proc append data = work._est_ base = work._est1_ force;run;
data work._fs_;
 set work._fs_;
 Ini = &i;
run;
proc append data = work._fs_ base = work._fs1_ force;run;
proc datasets library = work nolist;
 delete _est_ _fs_;
run;quit;


ods output AdditionalEstimates = work._est_ FitStatistics = work._fs_;
proc nlmixed data = work._in_ fd = central technique = quanew update = bfgs;
    by &by_vars;
```

```
parms a = &a, q = &q, delta = &delta, mu_b = &mu_b, mu_s =
&mu_s, ep_b = &ep_b, ep_s = &ep_s, D_b = &D_b, D_s = &D_s ;
    bounds 0 <= a <= 1, 0 <= q <= 1, 0 <= delta <= 1, mu_
b >= 0, mu_s >= 0, ep_b >= 0, ep_s >= 0, D_b >= 0, D_s >= 0;
    AdjPIN = ( a*((1-delta)*mu_b+delta*mu_s) )/( a*
((1-delta)*mu_b+delta*mu_s)+(D_b+D_s)*(a*q+(1-a)
*q)+ep_b+ep_s);
    PSOS = ( (D_b+D_s)*(a*q+(1-a)*q) )/( a*((1-delta)
*mu_b+delta*mu_s)+(D_b+D_s)*(a*q+(1-a)*q)+ep_b+
ep_s);
    Lik = (1-a)*(1-q)*pdf('poisson',&buy_var,ep_b)*pdf
('poisson',&sell_var,ep_s)+(1-a)*q*pdf('poisson',&buy_
var,(ep_b+D_b))*pdf('poisson',&sell_var,(ep_s+D_s))
     +a*(1-q)*delta*pdf('poisson',&buy_var,ep_b)*pdf
('poisson',&sell_var,(mu_s + ep_s))+a*q*delta*pdf
('poisson',&buy_var,(ep_b+D_b))*pdf('poisson',&sell_var,
(mu_s+ep_s+D_s))
     +a*(1-q)*(1-delta)*pdf('poisson',&buy_var,(mu_b
+ep_b))*pdf('poisson',&sell_var,ep_s)+a*q*(1-delta)
*pdf ('poisson', &buy_var, (mu_b + ep_b + D_b))*pdf
('poisson',&sell_var,(ep_s+D_s));
    if Lik = 0 then Lik = 1E-300;
    LogLik = log(Lik);
    model &buy_var~general ( LogLik );
    estimate 'alpha' a;
    estimate 'theta' q;
    estimate 'delta' delta ;
```

```
    estimate 'buy_mu' mu_b;
    estimate 'sell_mu' mu_s;
    estimate 'buy_epsilon' ep_b;
    estimate 'sell_epsilon' ep_s;
    estimate 'buy_CapitalDelta' D_b;
    estimate 'sell_CapitalDelta' D_s;
    estimate 'AdjPIN' adjpin;
    estimate 'PSOS' PSOS;
run;
data work._est_;
  set work._est_;
  Ini = &i;
run;
    proc append data = work._est_ base = work._est2_ force;run;
    data work._fs_;
      set work._fs_;
      Ini = &i;
    run;
    proc append data = work._fs_ base = work._fs2_ force;run;
    proc datasets library = work nolist;
      delete _est_ _fs_;
    run;quit;
%end;
    sasfile work._in_ close;
```

```
/* -------------Compile Results ------------- */
proc sql;
 create table work._final_ as
 select *
 from work._fs1_
 where Descr = '-2 Log Likelihood'
 order by &byvars2, value;
quit;
data work._final_;
 set work._final_;
 by &by_vars value;
 if first.&firstbyvar;
run;
proc sql;
 create table work._1_ as
 select a.*, 1 as Model
 from work._est1_ as a, work._final_ as b
 where &cond and a.Ini = b.Ini;
quit;
proc sql;
 create table work._final2_ as
 select *
 from work._fs2_
 where Descr = '-2 Log Likelihood'
 order by &byvars2, value;
quit;
data work._final2_;
```

```
  set work._final2_;
  by &by_vars value;
  if first.&firstbyvar;
run;
proc sql;
  create table work._2_ as
  select a.*, 2 as Model
  from work._est2_ as a, work._final2_ as b
  where &cond and a.Ini = b.Ini;
quit;

data work._3_;
  set work._1_ work._2_;
run;


data work._alpha1_ work._delta1_ work._mu1_ work._buy_
ep1_ work._sell_ep1_ work._Pin1_
        work._alpha2_ work._theta2_ work._delta2_ work._
buy_mu2_ work._sell_mu2_
        work._buy_ep2_ work._sell_ep2_ work._buy_capd2_
work._sell_capd2_ work._adjpin2_ work._psos2_;
    set work._3_;
   if Model = 1 then do;
     if Label = 'alpha' then output work._alpha1_;
     if Label = 'delta' then output work._delta1_;
     if Label = 'mu' then output work._mu1_;
     if Label = 'buy_epsilon' then output work._buy_ep1_;
```

```
      if Label ='sell_epsilon' then output work._sell_ep1_;
      if Label ='PIN' then output work._PIN1_;
    end;
    else do;
      if Label ='alpha' then output work._alpha2_;
      if Label ='theta' then output work._theta2_;
      if Label ='delta' then output work._delta2_;
      if Label ='buy_mu' then output work._buy_mu2_;
      if Label ='sell_mu' then output work._sell_mu2_;
      if Label ='buy_epsilon' then output work._buy_ep2_;
      if Label ='sell_epsilon' then output work._sell_ep2_;
      if Label = 'buy_CapitalD' then output work._buy_
capd2_;
      if Label = 'sell_Capital' then output work._sell_
capd2_;
      if Label ='AdjPIN' then output work._adjpin2_;
      if Label ='PSOS' then output work._psos2_;
    end;
  run;
  proc sort data =work._3_( keep =&by_vars ) out =work._
4_ nodupkey;
    by &by_vars;
  run;

  proc sql;
    create table &data_out as
    select a.*,
```

b. Estimate as Alpha1 Label = 'Alpha1: Prob Event Happens', b.StandardError as StdErr_Alpha1 Label = ' ', b.tValue as tValue_Alpha1 Label = ' ',

　　b.Probt as pValue_Alpha1 Label = ' ',

　　case when b.Probt > 0.1 then ' ' when 0.05 < b.Probt < = 0.1 then ' * ' when 0.01 < b.Probt < = 0.05 then ' * * ' else ' * * * ' end as Signif_Alpha1

　　from work._4_ as a left join work._alpha1_ as b

　　on &cond;

　　create table &data_out as

　　select a.*,

　　b.Estimate as Delta1 Label = 'Delta1: Prob Low Signal', b.StandardError as StdErr_Delta1 Label = ' ', b.tValue as tValue_Delta1 Label = ' ',

　　b.Probt as pValue_Delta1 Label = ' ',

　　case when b.Probt > 0.1 then ' ' when 0.05 < b.Probt < = 0.1 then ' * ' when 0.01 < b.Probt < = 0.05 then ' * * ' else ' * * * ' end as Signif_Delta1

　　from &data_out as a left join work._Delta1_ as b

　　on &cond;

　　create table &data_out as

　　select a.*,

　　b.Estimate as Mu1 Label = 'Mu1: Informed Order', b.StandardError as StdErr_Mu1 Label = ' ', b.tValue as tValue_Mu1 Label = ' ', b.Probt as pValue_Mu1 Label = ' ',

```
        case when b.Probt > 0.1 then '' when 0.05 < b.Probt <=
0.1 then '*' when 0.01 < b.Probt <= 0.05 then '**' else '*
**' end as Signif_Mu1
    from &data_out as a left join work._Mu1_ as b
    on &cond;


    create table &data_out as
    select a.*,
    b.Estimate as Buy_Epsilon1 Label = 'Buy_Epsilon1:
Uninformed Buy Order', b.StandardError as StdErr_Buy_Epsilon1
Label = '', b.tValue as tValue_Buy_Epsilon1 Label = '',
    b.Probt as pValue_Buy_Epsilon1 Label = '',
    case when b.Probt > 0.1 then '' when 0.05 < b.Probt <=
0.1 then '*' when 0.01 < b.Probt <= 0.05 then '**' else '*
**' end as Signif_Buy_Epsilon1
    from &data_out as a left join work._buy_ep1_ as b
    on &cond;


    create table &data_out as
    select a.*,
    b.Estimate as Sell_Epsilon1 Label = 'Sell_Epsilon1:
Uninformed Sell Order', b.StandardError as StdErr_Sell_
Epsilon1 Label = '', b.tValue as tValue_Sell_Epsilon1
Label = '',
    b.Probt as pValue_Sell_Epsilon1 Label = '',
    case when b.Probt > 0.1 then '' when 0.05 < b.Probt <=
0.1 then '*' when 0.01 < b.Probt <= 0.05 then '**' else '*
```

***' end as Signif_Sell_Epsilon1

from &data_out as a left join work._Sell_ep1_ as b

on &cond;

create table &data_out as

select a.*,

b.Estimate as PIN1 Label ='PIN1: PIN of Easley (1996)',
b.StandardError as StdErr_PIN1 Label =' ', b.tValue as tValue_PIN1 Label ='',

b.Probt as pValue_PIN1 Label ='',

case when b.Probt > 0.1 then '' when 0.05 < b.Probt <= 0.1 then '*' when 0.01 < b.Probt <= 0.05 then '**' else '***' end as Signif_PIN1

from &data_out as a left join work._PIN1_ as b

on &cond;

create table &data_out as

select a.*,

b. Estimate as Alpha2 Label = 'Alpha2: Prob Event Happens', b.StandardError as StdErr_Alpha2 Label ='', b.tValue as tValue_Alpha2 Label ='',

b.Probt as pValue_Alpha2 Label ='',

case when b.Probt > 0.1 then '' when 0.05 < b.Probt <= 0.1 then '*' when 0.01 < b.Probt <= 0.05 then '**' else '***' end as Signif_Alpha2

from &data_out as a left join work._alpha2_ as b

on &cond;

```
create table &data_out as
select a.*,
b.Estimate as Delta2 Label ='Delta2: Prob Low Signal',
b.StandardError as StdErr_Delta2 Label =' ', b.tValue as
tValue_Delta2 Label =' ',
b.Probt as pValue_Delta2 Label =' ',
case when b.Probt > 0.1 then ' 'when 0.05 < b.Probt < =
0.1 then '*' when 0.01 < b.Probt < = 0.05 then '* *' else '*
* *' end as Signif_Delta2
from &data_out as a left join work._Delta2_ as b
on &cond;

create table &data_out as
select a.*,
b.Estimate as Theta2 Label = 'Theta2: Prob Symmetric
Shock Happens', b.StandardError as StdErr_Theta2 Label =' ',
b.tValue as tValue_Theta2 Label =' ',
b.Probt as pValue_Theta2 Label =' ',
case when b.Probt > 0.1 then ' 'when 0.05 < b.Probt <=
0.1 then '*' when 0.01 < b.Probt <= 0.05 then '* *' else '* *
*' end as Signif_Theta2
from &data_out as a left join work._Theta2_ as b
on &cond;

create table &data_out as
select a.*,
b.Estimate as Buy_Mu2 Label = 'Buy_Mu2: Informed Buy
```

Order', b.StandardError as StdErr_Buy_Mu2 Label = ' ', b.tValue as tValue_Buy_Mu2 Label =' ',

　　b.Probt as pValue_Buy_Mu2 Label =' ',

　　case when b.Probt > 0.1 then ' ' when 0.05 < b.Probt <= 0.1 then '*' when 0.01 < b.Probt < = 0.05 then '* *' else '* * *' end as Signif_Buy_Mu2

　　from &data_out as a left join work._buy_mu2_ as b

　　on &cond;

　　create table &data_out as

　　select a.*,

　　b.Estimate as Sell_Mu2 Label ='Sell_Mu2: Informed Sell Order', b.StandardError as StdErr_Sell_Mu2 Label = ' ', b.tValue as tValue_Sell_Mu2 Label =' ',

　　b.Probt as pValue_Sell_Mu2 Label =' ',

　　case when b.Probt > 0.1 then ' ' when 0.05 < b.Probt <= 0.1 then '*' when 0.01 < b.Probt <= 0.05 then '* *' else '* * *' end as Signif_Sell_Mu2

　　from &data_out as a left join work._Sell_mu2_ as b

　　on &cond;

　　create table &data_out as

　　select a.*,

　　b.Estimate as Buy_Epsilon2 Label = 'Buy_Epsilon2: Uninformed Buy Order', b.StandardError as StdErr_Buy_Epsilon2 Label =' ', b.tValue as tValue_Buy_Epsilon2 Label =' ',

　　b.Probt as pValue_Buy_Epsilon2 Label =' ',

case when b.Probt > 0.1 then '' when 0.05 < b.Probt <= 0.1 then '*' when 0.01 < b.Probt <= 0.05 then '* *' else '* * *' end as Signif_Buy_Epsilon2

from &data_out as a left join work._buy_ep2_ as b

on &cond;

create table &data_out as

select a.*,

b.Estimate as Sell_Epsilon2 Label = 'Sell_Epsilon2: Uninformed Sell Order', b.StandardError as StdErr_Sell_Epsilon2 Label = ' ', b.tValue as tValue_Sell_Epsilon2 Label = '',

b.Probt as pValue_Sell_Epsilon2 Label = '',

case when b.Probt > 0.1 then '' when 0.05 < b.Probt <= 0.1 then '*' when 0.01 < b.Probt <= 0.05 then '* *' else '* * *' end as Signif_Sell_Epsilon2

from &data_out as a left join work._Sell_ep2_ as b

on &cond;

create table &data_out as

select a.*,

b.Estimate as Buy_CapDelta2 Label = 'Buy_CapDelta2: Increased Buy Order due to the Symmetric Shock', b.StandardError as StdErr_Buy_CapDelta2 Label = ' ', b.tValue as tValue_Buy_CapDelta2 Label = '',

b.Probt as pValue_Buy_CapDelta2 Label = '',

case when b.Probt > 0.1 then '' when 0.05 < b.Probt <=

0.1 then '*' when 0.01 < b.Probt < = 0.05 then '* *' else '* * *' end as Signif_Buy_CapDelta2

from &data_out as a left join work._buy_capd2_ as b on &cond;

create table &data_out as
select a.*,
b.Estimate as Sell_CapDelta2 Label = 'Sell_CapDelta2: Increased Sell Order due to the Symmetric Shock', b.StandardError as StdErr_Sell_CapDelta2 Label = ' ', b.tValue as tValue_Sell_CapDelta2 Label = ' ',
b.Probt as pValue_Sell_CapDelta2 Label = ' ',
case when b.Probt > 0.1 then ' ' when 0.05 < b.Probt <= 0.1 then '*' when 0.01 < b.Probt < = 0.05 then '* *' else '* * *' end as Signif_Sell_CapDelta2

from &data_out as a left join work._sell_capd2_ as b on &cond;

create table &data_out as
select a.*,
b. Estimate as AdjPIN2 Label = 'AdjPIN2: AdjPIN of Duarte (2009)', b.StandardError as StdErr_AdjPIN2 Label = ' ', b.tValue as tValue_AdjPIN2 Label = ' ',
b.Probt as pValue_AdjPIN2 Label = ' ',
case when b.Probt > 0.1 then ' ' when 0.05 < b.Probt < = 0.1 then '*' when 0.01 < b.Probt < = 0.05 then '* *' else '* * *' end as Signif_AdjPIN2

```
        from &data_out as a left join work._AdjPIN2_ as b
    on &cond;

    create table &data_out as
    select a.*,
        b.Estimate as PSOS Label='PSOS: An Illiquidity Proxy',
    b.StandardError as StdErr_PSOS Label=' ', b.tValue as
    tValue_PSOS Label=' ',
        b.Probt as pValue_PSOS Label=' ',
        case when b.Probt > 0.1 then ' ' when 0.05 < b.Probt <=
    0.1 then '*' when 0.01 < b.Probt <= 0.05 then '**' else '*
    **' end as Signif_PSOS
        from &data_out as a left join work._psos2_ as b
        on &cond
        order by &byvars ;
    quit;

    proc datasets library=work nolist;
        delete _alpha1__delta1__mu1__buy_ep1__sell_ep1__
    Pin1__alpha2__theta2__delta2__buy_mu2__sell_mu2__buy_
    ep2_
        _sell_ep2__buy_capd2__sell_capd2__adjpin2__psos2_
    _1__2__3__4__est1__est2__final__final2__fs1__fs2__ini
    __in_;
    run;quit;
    % mend PIN;
    % PIN (by_var2=Year, data_out=cnintra.PIN&year._a)
```

```
    % PIN ( by_var2 = SemiYear, data_out = cnintra.PIN&year.
_s)
    % PIN ( by_var2 = Quarter, data_out = cnintra.PIN&year._q)

    proc printto; run;
    ods listing;
    % put
    -----------------------------------------
----
    -----------------------------------------
----
    All jobs Finish at % sysfunc(putn(% sysfunc(datetime
()), datetime19.))
    -----------------------------------------
----
    -----------------------------------------
----;

    % mend baspin;
    % baspin (year =2004);
```

参 考 文 献

[1] Acharya, V. V., Pedersen, L. H. Asset Pricing with Liquidity Risk [J]. *Journal of Financial Economics*, 2005, 77 (2): 375-410.

[2] Amihud, Y., Mendelson, H. Liquidity and Stock Returns [J]. *Financial Analysts Journal*, 1986, 42 (3): 43-48.

[3] Bekaert, G., Harvey, C. R., Lundblad, C. Liquidity and Expected Returns: Lessons From Emerging Markets [J]. *Review of Financial Studies*, 2007, 20 (6): 1783-1831.

[4] Bernhardt, D., Hughson, E. Intraday Trade in Dealership Markets [J]. *European Economic Review*, 2002, 46 (9): 1697-1732.

[5] Brennan, M. J., Chordia, T., Subrahmanyam, A. Alternative Factor Specifications, Security Characteristics, and the Cross-Section of Expected Stock Returns [J]. *Journal of Financial Economics*, 1998, 49 (3): 345-373.

[6] Brennan, M. J., Subrahmanyam, A. Market Microstructure and Asset

Pricing: On the Compensation for Illiquidity in Stock Returns [J]. *Journal of Financial Economics*, 1996, 41 (3): 441 –464.

[7] Brown, K. C., Harlow, W. V., Starks, L. T. Of Tournaments and Temptations: An Analysis of Managerial Incentives in the Mutual Fund Industry [J]. *The Journal of Finance*, 1996, 51 (1): 85 –110.

[8] Brown, S. J., Goetzmann, W. N. Performance Persistence [J]. *The Journal of Finance*, 1995, 50 (2): 679 –698.

[9] Busse, J. A., Another Look at Mutual Fund Tournaments [J]. *Journal of Financial and Quantitative Analysis*, 2001, 36 (1): 53 –73.

[10] Carhart, M. M. On Persistence in Mutual Fund Performance [J]. *The Journal of Finance*, 1997, 52 (1): 57 –82.

[11] Chen, H., Pennacchi, G. G. Does Prior Performance Affect a Mutual Fund's Choice of Risk? Theory and Further Empirical Evidence [J]. *Journal of Financial and Quantitative Analysis*, 2009, 44 (4): 745 – 775.

[12] Chevalier, J., Ellison, G. Risk Taking by Mutual Funds as a Response to Incentives [J]. *Journal of Political Economy*, 1997, 105 (6): 1167 –1200.

[13] Dasgupta, A., Prat, A., Verardo, M. The Price Impact of Institutional Herding [J]. *Review of Financial Studies*, 2011, (Advance Access).

[14] Dass, N., Massa, M., Patgiri, R. Mutual Funds and Bubbles: The Surprising Role of Contractual Incentives [J]. *Review of Financial Studies*, 2008, 21 (1): 51 –99.

[15] Datar, V. T., Y. Naik, N., Radcliffe, R. Liquidity and Stock Returns: An Alternative Test [J]. *Journal of Financial Markets*, 1998, 1 (2): 203 –219.

[16] Del Guercio, D., Tkac, P. A. The Determinants of the Flow of Funds of Managed Portfolios: Mutual Funds Vs. Pension Funds [J]. *Journal of*

Financial and Quantitative Analysis, 2002, 37 (4): 523 – 557.

[17] Duarte, J., Young, L. Why is PIN Priced? [J]. *Journal of Financial Economics*, 2009, 91 (2): 119 – 138.

[18] Dybvig, P. H., Farnsworth, H. K., Carpenter, J. N. Portfolio Performance and Agency [J]. *Review of Financial Studies*, 2010, 23 (1): 1 – 23.

[19] Easley, D., Hvidkjaer, S., O'Hara, M. Is Information Risk a Determinant of Asset Returns? [J]. *The Journal of Finance*, 2002, 57 (5): 2185 – 2221.

[20] Easley, D., Kiefer, N. M., O'Hara, M., et al. Liquidity, Information, and Infrequently Traded Stocks [J]. *The Journal of Finance*, 1996, 51 (4): 1405 – 1436.

[21] Easley, D., O'Hara, M. Price, Trade Size, and Information in Securities Markets [J]. *Journal of Financial Economics*, 1987, 19 (1): 69 – 90.

[22] Easley, D., O'Hara, M. Information and the Cost of Capital [J]. *The Journal of Finance*, 2004, 59 (4): 1553 – 1583.

[23] Elton, E. J., Gruber, M. J., Blake, C. R. Survivor Bias and Mutual Fund Performance [J]. *Review of Financial Studies*, 1996, 9 (4): 1097 – 1120.

[24] Elton, E. J., Gruber, M. J., Blake, C. R. The Persistence of Risk – Adjusted Mutual Fund Performance [J]. *The Journal of Business*, 1996, 69 (2): 133 – 157.

[25] Elton, E. J., Gruber, M. J., Blake, C. R. Incentive Fees and Mutual Funds [J]. *The Journal of Finance*, 2003, 58 (2): 779 – 804.

[26] Fama, E. F., MacBeth, J. D. Risk, Return, and Equilibrium: Empirical Tests [J]. *Journal of Political Economy*, 1973, 81 (3): 607 – 636.

[27] George, T. J., Kaul, G., Nimalendran, M. Estimation of the Bid – Ask Spread and its Components: A New Approach [J]. *Review of Financial*

Studies, 1991, 4 (4): 623 – 656.

[28] Gibson, S., Safieddine, A., Sonti, R. Smart Investments by Smart Money: Evidence From Seasoned Equity Offerings [J]. *Journal of Financial Economics*, 2004, 72 (3): 581 – 604.

[29] Glosten, L. R., Harris, L. E. Estimating the Components of the Bid/Ask Spread [J]. *Journal of Financial Economics*, 1988, 21 (1): 123 – 142.

[30] Glosten, L. R., Milgrom, P. R. Bid, Ask and Transaction Prices in a Specialist Market with Heterogeneously Informed Traders [J]. *Journal of Financial Economics*, 1985, 14 (1): 71 – 100.

[31] Goetzmann, W. N., Ibbotson, R. G. Do Winners Repeat? Patterns in Mutual Fund Behavior [J]. *Journal of Portfolio Management*, 1994, 20 (2): 9 – 18.

[32] Goetzmann, W. N., Peles, N. Cognitive Dissonance and Mutual Fund Investors [J]. *Journal of Financial Research*, 1997, 20 (2): 145.

[33] Goriaev, A., Nijman, T. E., Werker, B. J. M. Yet Another Look at Mutual Fund Tournaments [J]. *Journal of Empirical Finance*, 2005, 12 (1): 127 – 137.

[34] Grinblatt, M., Titman, S. Mutual Fund Performance: An Analysis of Quarterly Portfolio Holdings [J]. *The Journal of Business*, 1989, 62 (3): 393 – 416.

[35] Grinblatt, M., Titman, S. The Persistence of Mutual Fund Performance [J]. *The Journal of Finance*, 1992, 47 (5): 1977 – 1984.

[36] Grinblatt, M., Titman, S. Performance Measurement without Benchmarks: An Examination of Mutual Fund Returns [J]. *The Journal of Business*, 1993, 66 (1): 47 – 68.

[37] Grinblatt, M., Titman, S., Wermers, R. Momentum Investment Strategies, Portfolio Performance, and Herding: A Study of Mutual Fund Behavior [J]. *American Economic Review*, 1995, 85 (5): 1088 – 1105.

[38] Gruber, M. J. Another Puzzle: The Growth in Actively Managed Mutual Funds [J]. *The Journal of Finance*, 1996, 51 (3): 783 – 810.

[39] Hendricks, D., Patel, J., Zeckhauser, R. Hot Hands in Mutual Funds: Short-Run Persistence of Relative Performance, 1974 – 1988 [J]. *The Journal of Finance*, 1993, 48 (1): 93 – 130.

[40] Hjalmarsson, E. New Methods for Inference in Long-Horizon Regressions [J]. *Journal of Financial and Quantitative Analysis*, 2011, 46 (3): 815 – 839.

[41] Ho, T., Stoll, H. R. Optimal Dealer Pricing Under Transactions and Return Uncertainty [J]. *Journal of Financial Economics*, 1981, 9 (1): 47 – 73.

[42] Huang, R. D., Stoll, H. R. The Components of the Bid-Ask Spread: A General Approach [J]. *Review of Financial Studies*, 1997, 10 (4): 995 – 1034.

[43] Ippolito, R. A. Consumer Reaction to Measures of Poor Quality: Evidence from the Mutual Fund Industry [J]. *Journal of Law and Economics*, 1992, 35 (1): 45 – 70.

[44] Kolari, J. W., Pynnönen, S. Event Study Testing with Cross-Sectional Correlation of Abnormal Returns [J]. *Review of Financial Studies*, 2010, 23 (11): 3996 – 4025.

[45] Korajczyk, R. A., Sadka, R. Pricing the Commonality Across Alternative Measures of Liquidity [J]. *Journal of Financial Economics*, 2008, 87 (1): 45 – 72.

[46] Kosowski, R., Timmermann, A., Wermers, R., et al. Can Mutual Fund "Stars" Really Pick Stocks? New Evidence From a Bootstrap Analysis [J]. *The Journal of Finance*, 2006, 61 (6): 2551 – 2595.

[47] Lee, C. M. C., Ready, M. J. Inferring Trade Direction From Intraday Data [J]. *The Journal of Finance*, 1991, 46 (2): 733 – 746.

[48] Lin, J., Sanger, G. C., Booth, G. G. Trade Size and Components of the Bid–Ask Spread [J]. Review of Financial Studies, 1995, 8 (4): 1153–1183.

[49] Lynch, A. W., Musto, D. K. How Investors Interpret Past Fund Returns [J]. The Journal of Finance, 2003, 58 (5): 2033–2058.

[50] MacKinlay, A. C. Event Studies in Economics and Finance [J]. Journal of Economic Literature, 1997, 35 (1): 13–39.

[51] Madhavan, A., Richardson, M., Roomans, M. Why Do Security Prices Change? A Transaction–Level Analysis of NYSE Stocks [J]. Review of Financial Studies, 1997, 10 (4): 1035–1064.

[52] Massa, M., Patgiri, R. Incentives and Mutual Fund Performance: Higher Performance or Just Higher Risk Taking? [J]. Review of Financial Studies, 2009, 22 (5): 1777–1815.

[53] Neal, R., Wheatley, S. M. Adverse Selection and Bid–Ask Spreads: Evidence From Closed–End Funds [J]. Journal of Financial Markets, 1998, 1 (1): 121–149.

[54] O'Hara, M. Presidential Address: Liquidity and Price Discovery [J]. The Journal of Finance, 2003, 58 (4): 1335–1354.

[55] O'Hara, M., Oldfield, G. S. The Microeconomics of Market Making [J]. Journal of Financial and Quantitative Analysis, 1986, 21 (4): 361–376.

[56] Pástor, Stambaugh, R. F. Liquidity Risk and Expected Stock Returns [J]. Journal of Political Economy, 2003, 111 (3): 642–685.

[57] Petersen, M. A. Estimating Standard Errors in Finance Panel Data Sets: Comparing Approaches [J]. Review of Financial Studies, 2009, 22 (1): 435–480.

[58] Sadka, R. Momentum and Post–Earnings–Announcement Drift Anomalies: The Role of Liquidity Risk [J]. Journal of Financial Economics, 2006, 80

(2): 309 – 349.

[59] Scharfstein, D. S., Stein, J. C. Herd Behavior and Investment [J]. *American Economic Review*, 1990, 80 (3): 465 – 479.

[60] Sias, R. W. Institutional Herding [J]. *The Review of Financial Studies*, 2004, 17 (1): 165 – 206.

[61] Sirri, E. R., Tufano, P. Costly Search and Mutual Fund Flows [J]. *The Journal of Finance*, 1998, 53 (5): 1589 – 1622.

[62] Stoll, H. R. Presidential Address: Friction [J]. *The Journal of Finance*, 2000, 55 (4): 1479 – 1514.

[63] Thompson, S. B. Simple Formulas for Standard Errors that Cluster by Both Firm and Time [J]. *Journal of Financial Economics*, 2011, 99 (1): 1 – 10.

[64] Van Ness, B. F., Van Ness, R. A., Warr, R. S. How Well Do Adverse Selection Components Measure Adverse Selection? [J]. *Financial Management*, 2001, 30 (3): 77 – 98.

[65] Wermers, R. Mutual Fund Herding and the Impact On Stock Prices [J]. *The Journal of Finance*, 1999, 54 (2): 581 – 622.

[66] Wermers, R. Mutual Fund Performance: An Empirical Decomposition Into Stock-Picking Talent, Style, Transactions Costs, and Expenses [J]. *The Journal of Finance*, 2000, 55 (4): 1655 – 1703.

[67] Zwiebel, J. Corporate Conservatism and Relative Compensation [J]. *Journal of Political Economy*, 1995, 103 (1): 1 – 25.